Meet the People Who Met Jesus

Meet the People Who Met Jesus: Encounters with Christ That Changed Lives

Copyright © 2025 John A. Cherico
ISBN 13: 979-8-218-72215-9
Library of Congress Control Number: 2025913775
Cover Photo: "Silhouette of a Well" by percds from Getty Images Signature for Canva
Cover design and layout by Helen Ounjian
Edited by Elizabeth Boerner
Perfect Misfits, LLC, An Independent Publishing Company
PerfectMisfits.DE@gmail.com

Perfect Misfits, LLC
An Independent Publishing Company

# Meet the PEOPLE Who Met JESUS

## Encounters with Christ That Changed Lives

John A. Cherico

I dedicate this book to my beautiful wife, Deb, my friend, lover, and partner in ministry and life. Every day is filled with your absence. Someday, we'll be together again, forever.

# Introduction

WHAT MAKES THIS BOOK A MUST-READ FOR YOU? It contains well-known biblical stories, offering life-changing truths that nourish the soul. I aim to provide a fresh perspective by exploring the emotional impact of individual conversations, often heightened by cultural context. I want the characters to leap off the page and engage the reader, fostering a deeper, life-altering application. I want you to see yourself standing beside those who encounter Christ for the first time, realizing that their struggles mirror your own and their needs reflect your current challenges.

Jesus was a master storyteller for good reason. Stories allow us to frame life within a context of definitive understanding. I invite you to stand with those who watched Jesus in action, sensing the amazement of His miracles while feeling the weight of His words. I want you to experience the same hope and healing that these biblical characters embraced when they met Jesus of Nazareth for the first time.

In the section entitled "Meet the People Who Met Jesus Today," you will find stories gathered from my daily encounters with incarcerated men and women. Many of these individuals are sinking into hopelessness and drowning in fearful apprehension. That is, until the light of God's loving and forgiving grace shines and embraces them. Marvel with me as the Spirit of God rescues these individuals from the brink of despair. The lessons here are simple. If the Lord can bring His light of forgiveness and grace to this dark and dismal place, He can reach and rescue anyone, anywhere.

This text allows you to choose which chapters to explore, and the chapters can be accessed in any order. Throughout this book, you will find questions at the end of each chapter designed to deepen personal Bible study and assist small group facilitators in guiding their members on a journey of spiritual growth and understanding.

I truly hope that as you read this, your relationship with the One who desires a close connection with you grows stronger, and that you'll discover the Way to the Father through your relationship with Christ.

# Table of Contents

## Meet the People Who Met Jesus Today: Blessings Behind Bars

# Encounter with the Samaritan Woman

John 4:1-26

*Now Jesus learned that the Pharisees had heard that He was gaining and baptizing more disciples than John— although in fact it was not Jesus who baptized, but His disciples. So He left Judea and went back once more to Galilee.*

*Now He had to go through Samaria. So He came to a town in Samaria called Sychar, near the plot of ground Jacob had given to his son Joseph. Jacob's well was there, and Jesus, tired as He was from the journey, sat down by the well. It was about noon.*

*When a Samaritan woman came to draw water, Jesus said to her, "Will you give Me a drink?" (His disciples had gone into the town to buy food.) The Samaritan woman said to Him, "You are a Jew and I am a Samaritan woman. How can You ask me for a drink?" (For Jews do not associate with Samaritans.) Jesus answered her, "If you knew the gift of God and who it is that asks you for a drink, you would have asked Him and He would have given you living water."*

*"Sir," the woman said, "You have nothing to draw with and the well is deep. Where can you get this living water? Are you greater than our father Jacob, who gave us the well and drank from it himself, as did also his sons and his livestock?" Jesus answered, "Everyone who drinks this water will be thirsty again, but whoever drinks the water I give them will never thirst. Indeed, the water I give them will become in them a spring of water welling up to eternal life." The woman said to Him, "Sir, give me this water so that I won't get thirsty and have to keep coming here to draw water."*

*He told her, "Go, call your husband and come back."*

*"I have no husband," she replied. Jesus said to her, "You are right when you say you have no husband. The fact is, you have had five husbands, and the man you now have is not your husband. What you have just said is quite true."*

*"Sir," the woman said, "I can see that You are a prophet. Our ancestors worshiped on this mountain, but you Jews claim that the place where we must worship is in Jerusalem."*

*"Woman," Jesus replied, "believe Me, a time is coming when you will worship the Father neither on this mountain nor in Jerusalem. You Samaritans worship what you do not know; we worship what we do know, for salvation is from the Jews. Yet a time is coming and has now come when the true worshipers will worship the Father in the Spirit and in truth, for they are the kind of worshipers the Father seeks. God is Spirit, and His worshipers must worship in the Spirit and in truth.*

*The woman said, "I know that Messiah (called Christ) is coming. When He comes, He will explain everything to us."*

*Then Jesus declared, "I, the one speaking to you—I am He."*

John 4:1-26

IT WAS HOT. Sweat dripped off your neck, sliding down your back—kind of hot. The sun's scorching rays cooked the ground beneath your feet, warming the dirt. There was no shade. No tent-like canopy to shield you from the blistering rays of the noonday sun. So, when you arrive at the well, you either stand there and sweat or sit on the edge of the well and sweat. This is what Jesus does as He waits for His disciples to return from town with food. But Jesus is where He is for another reason. Verse 4 says: **Now He had to go through Samaria.** Typically, Jews sidestep Samaria at all costs, willing to travel 100 miles out of the way to avoid contact. But Jesus **had to go through Samaria** because there was someone He wanted to meet. Someone Jesus wanted to talk to.

Well, it didn't take long before that someone, a woman carrying a water jug, came from the nearby village. She appeared on the crest of the hill, stopping briefly to wipe the sweat from her eyes with the back of her free hand. She felt annoyed when she saw a man sitting at the well. She came to *this* well, outside of town, at *this* time of day, to avoid people. But there he was, sitting on the edge of the well. Since she was out of water, she couldn't turn around. She had little to drink— not enough to wash her clothes or dishes— so she moved forward cautiously. The closer she got, the more she noticed that this wasn't just any man; He was a Jew! With that, the hair on the back of her neck stood up in contempt because the Samaritans and the Jews had a longstanding feud.

Over the years, the Jewish Samaritans intermarried with other groups who introduced them to false gods, which blended into the Samaritans' version of Judaism. Eventually, the Samaritans cleaned up their act and found their way back to the one true God.

However, they also had a different approach to God's Word. They only accept the first five books of the Scriptures but reject all the others. So, when the Jews come out of exile and begin to rebuild the temple, the Samaritans offer to help.

However, due to the Samaritans' past and their approach to the Scriptures, the Jews reject their offer. Later, when the Samaritans built their own temple, the Jews burned it down in 128 B.C. The Jews refer to the Samaritans as dogs—not the domesticated kind, but wild, mangy scavengers that prowl the countryside. Over time, the animosity between these groups evolved into full-blown hatred.

Now, the woman walking toward the well is a different breed. She isn't about to sit up and beg for any man, especially a Jewish one. Without a doubt, this woman's bite is worse than her bark. But who is she, really? This woman had dreams. She had romantic ambitions and fairy tale wishes. She hoped a handsome someone would sweep her off her feet. Instead, she endured a series of bad relationships. She has had five husbands and is now living with a sixth man. This causes her dreams to fade, replaced by the belief that true love is a myth.

Due to her history of broken relationships, her reputation in the community is less than stellar. Some wives notice their husbands giving her a look when she passes by. Believing this woman is a threat puts these wives on high alert. When this woman comes to the marketplace, bartering with a shopkeeper over prices, the shopkeeper's wife stands beside her husband, glaring at this homewrecker. But how did Jesus see her? He knows all about her. He knows she's lost and needs saving. However, Christ sees the raw potential in this woman. Similarly, when the Savior sees us, He knows who we are and what we've done. But Jesus also sees who we can become.

Notice how Jesus approaches her in verse 7, **When the Samaritan woman came to draw water, Jesus said to her, "Will you give Me a drink?"** When you go to someone's house that you don't know and they don't know you, you knock on the door or ring the bell, then take a step back. This way, you're not perceived as a threat.

When we approach someone with the Gospel, we should not step up and look down on them. Instead, we should step back into a non-threatening posture of humility. Missionary D.T. Niles once said that evangelism is "one beggar telling another beggar when to find food." Jesus' unassuming approach easily solicits a response from the woman, but her reply flashes with resentment over how the Jews treat her people. The Samaritan woman snaps back at Jesus, saying, **"You are a Jew, and I am a Samaritan woman."** (Can you feel the heat in her words?) **"How can you ask me for a drink?"**

People remember how you treat them and how you treat others. It leaves a reference point in their memory, categorized under aggression. This can happen when you're driving to church on Sunday. The person ahead of you is driving very slowly. They're not using their turn signals. They're just meandering around. You want to pass them or contemplate doing the unthinkable—blowing your horn. I know, only people from New York blow their horn like me. When I learned to drive out east, I had one hand on the steering wheel and one hand on the horn, always. I consider horn blowing a therapeutic tool, an instrument for behavior modification. Anyway, the person in front of you is still driving slowly when suddenly they turn into the same church parking lot you're pulling into. (Aren't you glad you didn't...?)

As I mentioned, Jesus' meeting with the Samaritan woman isn't accidental; *it's intentional,* which proves this fact, **wherever you are, Jesus can find you.** Some of you have family or friends who have walked away from God or who don't know the Lord at all.

You have been praying for them for a long time. Don't stop. Jesus *knows* where they are. When the time is right, a divine appointment will happen. Your prayers are vital for reaching them. I saw this happen in my family.

Friends of my older brother and his wife prayed for them for 25 years. Eventually, my brother and his wife, along with their children, were saved. Then, in her sixties, my mother was saved. My brother and his wife led me to the Lord.

Then my 75-year-old grandmother came to Christ. I led my wife to the Lord, and our four children were saved. My wife's parents, along with her two sisters, her brother, and some of their children, also came to Christ. I had the privilege of leading my father and stepmother to the Lord. The ripple effect of God's forgiving grace is a marvelous thing to witness. But it begins with the prayers of you and me. Don't give up.

Keep praying. Jesus *knows* who the lost in your family are. When the time is right, Christ will find them.

In verse 10, Jesus doesn't take the bait; instead, He redirects the conversation with this statement: ***"If you knew the gift of God and who it is that asks you for a drink, you would have asked Him, and He would have given you living water."*** At this point, the Samaritan woman bites down on her lower lip as she contemplates Jesus' words. But what is this 'gift of God' Jesus is offering? Ephesians 2:8 gives us the answer: ***For it is by grace you have been saved, through faith—and this not from yourselves, it is the gift of God.*** In this encounter, Jesus embodies the living, breathing grace of God in action. Keep in mind that this woman, in this obscure, hot place, in the middle of the day, wants nothing to do with anybody. And yet, God wants everything to do with her. A person will encounter Jesus when the time is right. So, keep praying.

In John 4:11-12, the Samaritan woman takes an assertive stance. It's like a one-two punch aimed at Jesus. First, she makes a subtle jab suggesting that the Savior is unprepared to retrieve water, which puts His offer of 'Living Water' in jeopardy. ***"Sir,"*** **the woman said,** ***"You have nothing to draw with, and the well is deep. Where can you get this living water?"*** Assuming the water is from the well, the woman completely misses Christ's reference.

Then the Samaritan woman lashes out with a putdown. ***"Are you greater than our father Jacob, who gave us the well and drank from it himself, as did also his sons and his flocks and herds?"*** Even today, the Samaritans define themselves as descendants of the tribe of Joseph, one of the 12 sons of Jacob. Today, there remains a small enclave of Samaritans living on the West Bank. These descendants of the Samaritan woman form a splinter group wedged between the Jews and Palestinians.

But again, Jesus refuses to engage in a cultural argument. Instead, He points to the well and says, Everyone who drinks this water will be thirsty again, but whoever drinks the water I give them will never thirst. Indeed, the water I give him will become in him a spring of water welling up to eternal life. Jesus is talking about the spiritual benefits of salvation that He offers. However, the Samaritan woman sees this as a solution for her need to come back for water in the future. ***"Sir, give me this water so I won't get thirsty and have to keep coming here to draw water"*** (verse 15). Now, this is the moment when things get interesting.

Jesus makes a statement that, on the surface, appears innocent enough. However, Christ's statement addresses the real problem in the woman's life. In verse 16, Jesus says, ***"Go call your husband and come back."*** Without wondering why her husband should get involved, she quickly blurts out, ***"I have no husband"*** (verse 17). Now, Christ gets to the heart of the issue because the Samaritan woman's broken heart is the issue. It's time to heal her wounded heart, which has resulted from her poor choices.

Never forget that sin always takes a toll, bringing shame and guilt to bear down on us. From the very beginning, sin drove Adam and Eve away from God, compelling them to hide in the bushes. We, too, can attempt to conceal ourselves behind the shrubbery of denial. We shift blame, point fingers, and create a list of excuses for our actions. Deep down, we're afraid that God will see us for who we really are because of what we do.

The truth is that the Lord already sees and knows who we are and what we've done. In fact, He knows what we will do before we do it. Our actions might shock us, but they're no surprise to God. When the Lord saves you, He has no illusions about who you are. God doesn't save us because we'll become perfect people; He saves us because we're not. We're sinners who can't save ourselves and people who will never be perfect in this life. However, we need to acknowledge and take ownership of our bad choices. Sin is serious because it can and will disrupt lives and destroy relationships. Now, the Samaritan woman wasn't innocent. She contributed to those five disastrous relationships, leaving her reputation in shambles. I'm sure that her view on life is tainted by these relational failures. I wonder if she had any friends.

Due to our mistakes, disappointments, and deep wounds, we can easily start believing that we're beyond hope or that someone we know seems to be beyond reach; it's simply not true. Here's why: **Whatever you've done, Jesus can forgive you.** There is no sin greater than God's grace. No life is beyond repair. No soul is beyond rescue. Honest repentance leads to full redemption. However, one thing that often stands in the way of receiving God's forgiveness is not asking for it.

Please understand that saving grace is not merely a gentle breeze blowing into your life. Sometimes, saving grace feels like a slap in the face because it serves as a wake-up call. This is what Jesus does in response to the woman's admission that she has no husband.

In response, Jesus says, ***"You are right when you say you have no husband. The fact is, you have had five husbands, and the man you now have is not your husband. What you just said is quite true"*** (verses 17-18). Saving grace is that moment when the Lord God slams on the stadium lights to reveal who you are, what you're doing, and why change is necessary. It was the theologian Augustine who wrote, "There is a God-shaped hole in the human heart that only God can fill."

I see that the God-shaped hole comes into view for inmates on a regular basis. Once locked up, they lose all freedom, shattering the illusion of being in control. They're told what to wear, when and what to eat, and when to sleep and wake up. When you reach the point where everything is taken from you, you realize that losing everything is possible, especially if you're on the wrong path.

This leads to the sobering conclusion that bad choices yield bad results. Frequently, inmates at the jail where I work come to this awareness by sending me messages like this: "I want God in my life, can you help me?" "I know that God brought me here to get my attention. What should I do?" "Please pray for me, I want to be right with God and myself."

Now, for people like us, it's more difficult to come to terms with our emptiness. We tend to fill that God-shaped hole with worldly things. Money, possessions, work, and even family can take God's place. These things aren't bad in and of themselves, except when they become a substitute for the Lord. When you allow anything to take God's place, especially addiction, you're in the worst place you can be. Eventually, life comes crashing down, alerting us that we're not in control, nor are we excluded from sorrow or exempt from pain. Tragedy can often be a mirror, showing us who we really are while exposing our true priorities. The Samaritan woman needed to own the mess in her life. At first, she doesn't appreciate Jesus pointing out the errors of her past.

She recognizes that Jesus has a special ability, calling Him a "Prophet" in verse 19. Then she goes on the offensive by referring to the ongoing conflict between the Samaritans and the Jews regarding places of worship in verse 20, *"Our ancestors worshiped on this mountain, but you Jews claim that the place where we must worship is in Jerusalem."*

The Savior quickly cuts through this age-old conflict by stating that it doesn't matter where you worship; what truly matters is how you worship God. *God is Spirit, and His worshippers must worship in Spirit and Truth* (John 4:24). This means it's not about rules and rituals; it's about having a relationship with the One True God through His Son Jesus, the Messiah.

This is a turning point, as it goes exactly where Jesus wants it to go. Verse 25, *The woman said, "I know the Messiah (called Christ) is coming. When He comes, He will explain everything to us." Then Jesus declared, "I who speak to you am He."* Never had Jesus openly revealed Himself to anyone. Not to John the Baptist, His disciples, or the religious leaders. But now, He reveals Himself to this Samaritan woman, this 5-time divorcee and social outcast. Why? Because Christ doesn't see us based on who we are or what we've done. Jesus sees who we can become. So far, we've learned that: **Wherever you are, Jesus can find you. Whatever you've done, Jesus can forgive you.** Now we learn: **Whoever you are, Jesus can use you.** In verse 27, the disciples return and are surprised to find that Jesus is talking to some woman in public. This is something no self-respecting Jew would ever do, especially since she's a Samaritan.

Seemingly disregarding the returning disciples and losing interest in fetching water, the Samaritan woman leaves her water jar by the well. She then hikes up her skirt, kicking up dust as she dashes back to town. What's amazing is that now, she seeks out the very people she wants to avoid.

No longer ashamed, this woman admits her wrongdoings as an incentive for people to come meet Jesus. Verse 29 ***"Come, see a man who told me everything I ever did. Could this be the Christ?"*** What the Samaritan woman says is both revealing and compelling. Whenever we climb down from the high horse of pride and choose to talk to each other in humble honesty, wonderful things happen. It's amazing that this despised and rejected woman becomes the first missionary.

This proves that the only thing you need to reach others is the truth: the truth about who Jesus is and how He changed you. You don't need to graduate from Bible college or have a seminary education. You don't even need a course in evangelism. What you need is to believe in the power of your conversion story, trusting that the same power that changed you can change others. Then, share your unique story with family and friends. Romans 10:14 asks this key question: And how can they hear about Jesus unless someone tells them?

You might be the answer to the prayers of family and friends who don't know Christ. If you believe the Lord can use you, then make yourself available to God by sharing the truth that changed you. But don't expect everyone to drop to their knees in repentance; not everyone will. Look at the results in John 4:39-41: ***Many of the Samaritans from that town believed in Him because of the woman's testimony, "He told me everything I ever did." So when the Samaritans came to Him, they urged Him to stay with them, and He*** *stayed 2 days. And because of His words, many more became believers.*

In the end, it's not about people believing in us. They must believe in Jesus. *Then they said to the woman, "We no longer believe because of what you said; now we have heard for ourselves, and we know this man really is the Savior of the world"* (John 4:42). John 3:17 affirms that this was always Jesus' divine mission. *For God did not send His Son into the world to condemn the world, but to save the world through Him.* Every person you see or know is precious in God's sight, created in His image and likeness. We should see people as the Lord does: either saved or lost. Nothing in between. Always remember that it doesn't matter who you are or what you've done.

God can find you, forgive you, and use you to share His truth with this lost and hurting world. Your story is uniquely special because it is yours.

No one can tell your story like you can because you lived it. Your story affirms that Almighty God is still in the soul-saving, life-changing business. You are proof positive that this is true. So, share your story so that others, just like you, can be set free, since everyone everywhere needs a Savior. This means our responsibility is to tell others about what our Savior has done for us.

## Chapter 1 Questions

1. We often 'rush to judgment' with people based solely on a glance. How can we break this habit?

2. How does gossip about someone damage their reputation and alter our perceptions of them?

3. Sometimes we come across angry people—individuals with an attitude. What could be the cause of this behavior?

4. Why do people think they can fix, change, or even save themselves spiritually?

5. The Samaritan woman has an 'axe to grind' with the Jews. How does Jesus steer clear of arguing with her?

6. Is it true that a saving grace can be a slap in the face? If so, could you please explain?

7. If everyone has a 'God-shaped hole' in their heart, how do people attempt to fill it?

8. Why is your testimony (your salvation story) so important?

# Healing the Man with Leprosy

Matthew 8:1-4

*When Jesus came down from the mountainside, large crowds followed Him. A man with leprosy came and knelt before Him and said, "Lord, if You are willing, you can make me clean."*

*Jesus reached out His hand and touched the man. "I am willing," He said. "Be clean!" Immediately he was cleansed of his leprosy.*

*Then Jesus said to him, "See that you don't tell anyone. But go, show yourself to the priest and offer the gift Moses commanded, as a testimony to them."*

Matthew 8:1-4

THE HEADING IN MY BIBLE labels this portion of Scripture as "The man with leprosy." This is who he is at that moment. But who was he, really? Well, he could have been a merchant who opened his shop early every day. His wife came to help him sell their vegetables while their children played in the back. He might have been a farmer who stopped to wipe his sweaty brow on a hot, sunny day; then, looking up, he sees his family coming toward him, carrying his lunch. Maybe he was a craftsman with a reputation for being skilled and honest. His kids, a boy and a girl, would help him sweep up his shop at the end of each day. He's just an average guy whose world suddenly falls apart. What started as a rash didn't respond to any home remedy. Eventually, this rash turned into an open, oozing sore that spread. So, he sleeps outside on the flat roof of his house just to play it safe. But he will never come inside again because one day, a local healer gives him the sad news: leprosy.

At that moment, the color drains from his wife's face, and his kids become confused and start crying when their father walks away, with only the clothes on his back. The man walks away in a dazed confusion, trying to process this terrible news. This is when this average, hardworking family man joins the ranks of the original walking dead.

Men and women plagued by this terrible disease of leprosy endure a lifetime of social isolation, physical disfigurement, and unending pain. Some say that misery loves company. Could this be why people with leprosy congregate? Not that they can help or support each other much; they can't. Is there strength in numbers? Not with this group. The only thing they can do is keep each other company in their heartache. They stay together since no one else wants them around. The healthy masses ensure this disease-ridden group maintains their distance. Out of sight, out of mind, and certainly out of reach. In fact, by law, people with leprosy must keep a 16 ft. distance from others, crying out, 'Unclean, Unclean' if anyone approaches. They sometimes wear bells to sound the alarm, so others can be safe. They also wear veils to hide the terrible erosion of skin, lips, and sometimes even a nose.

Occasionally, a kind soul would leave food for the people with leprosy on the outskirts of town. However, eating and drinking are never easy, especially with scabs on your lips and sores inside your mouth. Furthermore, handling food is difficult with claw-like hands due to muscle and nerve damage.

Usually, the local inhabitants chase away people with leprosy. But it's hard to run when all you can do is hobble, using a tree branch as a cane or crutch. It's even harder to feel the painful thud of rejection when you're hit in the back with rocks. Even animals keep their distance, deterred by the smell of disease and the stench of decay. This is hardly a life worth living; it's an unbearable existence devoid of family, friends, and hope.

Imagine, if you can, the scene of their final goodbye. The leper's wife brings both children to the edge of town.

They stand at a safe distance from the diseased man. But this diseased man is Daddy. So, the kids want to run up and hug him. They haven't seen him for a while and miss him. But this mother holds a firm grip on her children.

Contact with their leper father would expose them to this horrible disease. Still, the kids squeal and squirm, trying to break free. Tears stream down the wife's face. In heart-wrenching desperation, she turns away and walks off. The kids are frantic, almost hysterical, as their mother pulls them away. The little boy goes limp in protest, forcing the mother to scoop him up. Looking back over his mother's shoulder, the little boy cries out, "Daddy," while waving a weak goodbye. Even after they leave, the man stands there for a long time. He knows this will be the last time he sees his family. Sometimes disease does more than damage the body; it can also drain your heart of hope.

So, with this imaginative backstory in place, the encounter between Jesus and the leper unfolds in Luke 5:12. **While Jesus was in one of the towns, a man appeared who was covered with leprosy.** It sounds like a chance encounter, doesn't it? But was it? Not likely. It was as coincidental as Jesus choosing Simon Peter's boat as his pulpit. As random as Christ waiting at the well for the Samaritan woman. As accidental as the thief turning to the Savior on the cross, or the Risen Savior chasing down two heartbroken disciples on the Emmaus Road.

Proverbs 16:9 NLT makes it clear: We can make our plans, but the Lord determines our steps. God always seeks to draw us to Himself.

Now, when the Savior encounters the diseased man, we do not know how long he has been sick, but we do know he is entombed within this all-consuming disease. In various Bible versions, his condition is described consistently. He is described as *"covered with leprosy,"* having an *"advanced case of leprosy,"* and experiencing *"disease all over his body."* This man is awash in pain and suffering because he is *"full of leprosy."* All these descriptions underscore the fact that he is plagued by a full-blown epidemic spreading over his entire body. The horror of this disease has transformed him into someone with deformed features.

This could be why he tries to conceal his appearance when approaching Christ. In Luke 5:12, ...**When he saw Jesus, he fell with his face to the ground and begged him, "Lord, if You are willing, You can make me clean."**

So, can you imagine the disciples' reaction when the leper charges forward? They were climbing over one another, trying to back up and get away. But Jesus never backs down. We're told that Jesus eventually reaches out and touches the man. Clearly, there wasn't 16 feet between them. No matter what we've done, where we've been, or what we have become, Jesus steps up to meet us exactly where we are. Nothing prevents the Lord God from finding us, loving us, and saving us. The Savior steps up in the same way He steps down into this mess of a world.

For this reason, Christ allows Himself to die on the cross as a symbol of healing and hope that delivers salvation to anyone who believes. Are you plagued by something that hurts you? Jesus can heal you. You might be trapped in the misery of certain habits. Jesus can set you free. However, it won't happen randomly; it only occurs intentionally. We must be willing participants in this experience. The Lord God will never force Himself upon us because He desires that we genuinely want Him. Therefore, we must come to God, cry out to Him, and always ask, believing in faith. That's what the leper does. When we do this, Almighty God is ready to respond. But we should be mindful that our prayers should never be flavored with the belief that God will grant exactly what we ask when we request it. Don't pray, "Lord, I need this now; by the way, I need it ASAP." Be careful not to treat the Lord like a celestial Santa Claus.

Let's learn from the leper when he approaches Jesus in verse 12. He says, *"Lord, if you are willing, you can make me clean."* There is no doubt in the leper's mind that Jesus can heal him. However, he doesn't assume that Christ is *willing* to do so. This seems strange, doesn't it? It raises the question, how open-ended are our prayers? Are they contingent upon the Lord giving us what we want? Or are we willing to pray, "Lord, I know you are able, but are You willing?"

But even if you're not, I'm okay with that. It's not easy to pray that way. This approach acknowledges that God's plans and ways are not always ours.

I was recently ministering to an inmate charged with a violent crime. It took a while for Bob to express himself. You see, Bob is dying from stage 4 throat cancer, and hospice is involved. Unfortunately, Bob can't receive a 'mercy release' due to the seriousness of his crime. I visited Bob several times in our infirmary, but he struggles to communicate. His face is bright red and swollen, with one eye shut. His lips are bloated and seem ready to burst. They slide in opposite directions, distorting his features. A gap on the right side of his mouth frequently erupts with a spray of saliva. His neck muscles are so weak that he holds up his head with one hand. It's not easy to look at Bob. But we must strive to look beyond human weakness to catch a glimpse of a person's soul. This is what Jesus does. Eventually, I read Scripture to Bob and then explained its meaning. I shared with Bob the story about Nicodemus, where Jesus tells him, "You must be born again" (referenced in John 3:3). I was anxious to follow up in our next meeting. Bob also wanted a Bible, which I brought. Unfortunately, Bob was moved to a different facility that had a hospice unit an hour before we met again. I suppose Bob will get better care, but I was more than a little disappointed. I had invested time and prayer in Bob and asked others to pray for his salvation as well. I knew God was able to save him, but the Lord wasn't willing, at least not willing to do it my way. For this reason, we should pray open-ended prayers, acknowledging that God is always able, but sometimes He doesn't do what we want or expect. However, rest assured that the Lord always does what's best.

In the Old Testament, three young Israelites in Babylonian captivity learn this lesson the hard way. The story is found in Daniel 3:16-18. The King of Babylon makes a golden statue, requiring everyone to bow down and worship this image. Three young Jewish men, Shadrach, Meshach, and Abednego, refuse. King Nebuchadnezzar is outraged, threatening to throw them into a blazing furnace if they don't comply. Listen carefully to their response. ***Shadrach, Meshach, and Abednego replied to him, "King Nebuchadnezzar, we do not need to defend ourselves before you in this matter. If we are thrown into the blazing furnace, the God we serve is able to deliver us from it, and He will deliver us from Your Majesty's hand. But even if He does not, we want you to know, Your Majesty, that we will not serve your gods or worship the image of gold you have set up."***

Are you willing to accept that God is always able but not always willing? Do you understand that there are times when the Lord God does not give you what you want? Does He not help you when you ask? Does He not spare you from the trauma of this life? The Lord God is always able, but He's not always willing to do things our way. He's not always willing to spare us from the pain and suffering we want to avoid. Shadrach, Meshach, and Abednego aren't saved *from* the fiery furnace; they're saved *in* the fiery furnace. Likewise, Daniel isn't saved *from* the lion's den; he's saved *in* the lion's den. The disciples aren't saved *from* the storms but *in* them.

Trouble isn't an indication of God's neglect; rather, it is a sure sign of His participation. Sometimes, you must feel the heat of the fire or the hot breath of a lion on your neck. You may have to face the gale-force winds of the storm before the Lord God shows up. Please understand that the Lord doesn't sweep trauma out of your way. Instead, He takes your trauma and teaches you how to turn it into triumph. Isaiah 43:2-3 (NLT) confirms this: ***"When you go through deep waters, I will be with you. When you go through rivers of difficulty, you will not drown. When you walk through the fire of oppression, you will not be burned up; the flames will not consume you. For I am the LORD your God, the Holy One of Israel, your Savior."*** The only way to get through difficulty is to go through it; avoidance never works.

Avoidance is like running to an exit door, only to find it locked. This forces you to turn around and face what's in the room with you. So, what's in the room with you this morning? Whatever it is, rest assured, Jesus Christ is right there with you. Jesus will never abandon or disown you. He will help you through whatever you're facing.

In Matthew 8:3, we witness the dramatic moment when the miraculous takes center stage. It says, ***Jesus reached out His hand and touched the man.*** Why did Jesus touch him when it wasn't necessary? Jesus performed healing miracles on people who were far away. So why did the Savior touch the leper? This is what the Lord God does: He reaches down into the sewer of our existence, making us new creatures in Christ.

Let's not forget that this man has not been touched for who knows how long. The weight of Christ's hand on his shoulder signaled the beginning of his re-entry into society. It had to feel good. But the word 'touch' doesn't give us the full picture. In the original language, it means 'took hold of him' or 'embrace.' Yes, Jesus is willing to put himself at risk. Not risk from the disease, but risking what others might think of Him or how they might react to Him hugging a person with leprosy. Throughout His ministry, Jesus is accused of associating with the so-called misfits and public outcasts of society. Those labeled a lost cause. Know anyone like that? Those people were Christ's specialty.

So, to the leper, the Savior responds, (Matthew 8:3 continues), ***"I am willing." Jesus said, "Be clean!" And <u>immediately</u> he was cleansed of his leprosy.*** You see, this healing wasn't gradual; it was immediate. Each and every sore that was there before wasn't there anymore. If there were missing fingers, toes, or a nose, they suddenly reappeared where they belonged. Bones became strong. Muscles were pumped with renewed vitality. The smell of disease and the stench of decay were replaced by the sweet aroma of clean, fresh skin. Then a man who had been face down on the ground.

It is written in Luke 5:14, ***Then Jesus ordered him, "Don't tell anyone, but go, show yourself to the priest and offer the sacrifices that Moses commanded for your cleansing, as a testimony to them."*** He stands up, ready to embrace his new life. All his pain and suffering will be behind him. How do you think his family will react? What will he say to them?

There were specific steps the Law required for someone to reenter the community, especially when health issues were in question. Ceremonial washing, followed by shaving one's head, beard, and even eyebrows, is necessary. After more washing and a change of clothes, sacrifices are to be offered in the temple. Why was Jesus so emphatic about his instructions? The answer is found in the last five words of Luke 5:14, ***"...as a testimony to them."*** Jesus is using His healing miracle to reach the priests in the temple. Christ never gave up on the religious elite, even though they never gave Him a chance. Jesus was trying to open their hearts despite their closed minds. Christ wanted to give them life, while their response to Him was death. Did Jesus succeed? Acts 6:7 gives us the answer, ***So, the word of God spread. The number of disciples in Jerusalem increased rapidly, and a large number of priests became obedient to the faith.***

Despite this success, Jesus demonstrates that being right will not keep you off the cross. Trouble will come, but remember that trouble is not an indication of God's neglect. Rather, trouble is a sure sign of God's closeness. God's answer to this troubled world is Calvary's cross, the ultimate act of Divine participation, which changes human history.

This is why putting your faith in Jesus Christ will change the course of your life. Now let's not forget our friend, the former leper. He stands outside the door of his house, his hands sweaty and his stomach churning. He doesn't know why he's nervous, but he is.

He can hear his kids playing inside as his wife calls them, saying that dinner is almost ready. Well, it's now or never. Slowly, the man grips the handle and pushes the door open. Three heads turn just as he steps in. His wife gasps, and his kids look up in shock and disbelief. Remember, his hair, beard, and even his eyebrows have been shaved off. He must have been a strange sight. His kids freeze, and his wife stands still, holding a kitchen towel in both hands while holding her breath. Finally, he looks at them and says just two words: "Daddy's home!" They rush together into a group hug, followed by tears of joy. Only now is this healing miracle complete.

## Chapter 2 Questions

1. Have you ever experienced a time when illness or disease impacted your close relationships? If so, how and where?

2. People often refer to life events as unexpected circumstances. Some call this destiny. How should a Christian perceive the unexpected circumstances of life?

3. Is there anything standing between you and Jesus at this moment? If so, how will you go about removing it?

4. Open-ended prayers don't require specific answers to particular issues. Rather, they seek and embrace God's will above all else. Do you pray in this manner?

5.  We often pray to the Lord for protection from trouble. So, when we find ourselves in trouble, does that mean God has let us down?

6.  So, what kind of difficulties are you facing right now? How would praying 'open-ended prayers' affect the outcome? Are you willing to try?

7.  Do you know someone who might be considered a lost cause? What are your thoughts about them? What would Jesus want you to do for this person?

8.  When you consider the comprehensive healing power of this miracle, do you believe that Jesus can assist you with any problem you might be facing?

# The Widow of Nain

## Luke 7:11-17

*Soon afterward, Jesus went to a town called Nain, and His disciples and a large crowd went along with Him. As He approached the town gate, a dead person was being carried out—the only son of his mother, and she was a widow. And a large crowd from the town was with her. When the Lord saw her, His heart went out to her and He said, "Don't cry."*

*Then He went up and touched the bier (coffin) they were carrying him on, and the bearers stood still. He said, "Young man, I say to you, get up!" The dead man sat up and began to talk, and Jesus gave him back to his mother.*

*They were all filled with awe and praised God. "A great prophet has appeared among us," they said. "God has come to help His people." This news about Jesus spread throughout Judea and the surrounding country.*

Luke 7:11-17

AFTER BEING A PASTOR FOR OVER 30 YEARS, I've done my share of funerals. In one North Dakota funeral, we drove almost two hours north of Bismarck for the burial. I rode in the car carrying the casket of the deceased. It was winter, which meant the frozen gravesite had to be dug carefully and well in advance. Upon arriving, we discovered the wrong gravesite had been opened. So, we postponed the burial until spring. On the way back, the driver suggested we stop at the family farm, where a meal was prepared for anyone who attended the burial. It took me a while to convince him that it wouldn't be appropriate for us to chow down on pulled pork sandwiches and tater-tot hotdish while the recently departed was parked outside in the driveway. We drove back instead. The driver wasn't happy.

In another funeral, I rode with the family to the cemetery. I remember there wasn't much conversation as we drove—just the passing of tissues, quiet tears, and distant looks of shock and disbelief. As we traveled, I looked outside and noticed that everyone was continuing with life as usual. I saw a couple talking while walking their dog, smiling people riding bikes, and kids playing in a nearby park. But inside the car, time seemed to stand still. It was as if we were suspended somewhere between life and death.

Funerals can evoke a range of emotions, often stopping you dead in your tracks. This is what happens to Jesus, His disciples, and a large crowd as they approach the town of Nain. We understand why the disciples were with Jesus. However, this sizable group of hangers-on is something new. They had witnessed some of Christ's miracles back in Capernaum, prompting them to tag along in hopes of seeing more miraculous signs and wonders. This crowd is filled with expectation, while the crowd approaching them is filled with grief.

Nain is a small village in Galilee, located approximately 30 miles southwest of Capernaum, Jesus' residence during His earthly ministry. Nain is an out-of-the-way place in the middle of nowhere. To reach it, you embark on a challenging uphill climb on a narrow dirt road that leads to this tiny town. The word *Nain* means "beauty" or "pleasantness." Nain may have earned its name due to its location high on a hill, which offers a breathtaking view of the sunbaked plain of Carmel, the bronze hills of Nazareth, and the white peak of Mount Hermon glistening in the distance.

Nain was in a small farming community with a town too small to have a surrounding wall or a town gate. The gate mentioned was nothing more than the city's entrance between two buildings leading into the village center. Despite its modest existence, Nain becomes the setting for one of Jesus' most extraordinary miracles. Before we can examine the miracle, we must explore the background of this encounter. Once again, we read in verse 12: *As He* [Jesus] ***approached the town gate, a dead person was being carried out- the only son of his mother, and she was a widow. And a large crowd from the town was with her.***

In the first century, this solemn procession deserves the utmost respect. This causes the enthusiastic crowd with Jesus to grow quiet and still, while the sounds from the funeral crowd are low groans of grief. Public displays of mourning were encouraged in that culture, but this is not a performance. It's the noise of human pain bubbling up and spilling over. The Hebrew word for funeral is 'levaya,' which means 'to accompany.' The crowd is there to accompany the deceased to their burial while showing support for the family. There is only one relative present, a woman who is the mother of the deceased man. This woman is also a widow, so this isn't the first time she has walked in a funeral procession.

There was a terrible moment in the past when she buried her husband. We don't know when that was or how long they were married, but we can assume it was heartbreaking to lose her lifelong partner. Death is many things; most importantly, it is a thief, as it robs us of the well-meaning assurances we share with one another. Death nullifies the promises our loved ones make to us, like, "Honey, we'll be together for a long time; even when we're old, I'll hold your hand." Not so. Not once death arrives. However, when this woman walked in her husband's funeral procession, she wasn't alone. Her son stood beside her. When she became a little shaky on her feet, her son put his arm around her and said, "Don't worry Mom, we'll get through this together." At the graveside, when this woman was crying even harder, her son put his arm around her again and said, "Don't worry Mom, I'll take care of you." The young man did just that. He managed her financial affairs, keeping his mother safe and secure.

Even the neighbors remarked on how lucky this woman was to have a son like this. Well, she once had a son like that, but now this woman's only son is gone. We don't know how he died. All that really matters is that he's dead. Pallbearers carry his lifeless body on a litter as this woman leads the funeral procession. She's holding a wad of tear-soaked tissues in one hand while clutching her dress with the other, as if she's trying to hang on. This time, there isn't anyone to lean on. Her son's reassuring voice is silent, never to be heard again. She's out in front, feeling terribly vulnerable and alone. This grieving mother is followed by the pallbearers, who are friends of the young man and some helpful neighbors. The younger men watch the older ones for direction. They work hard to keep the stretcher level while maintaining a slow and respectful pace behind the woman, who is crying almost non-stop. This woman cries because she knows the promises her son made will be buried with him. Life has become sad and very scary for this woman.

Now, the people in this crowd have attended many funerals before. If you live in a small town where everyone knows each other, you attend more than your fair share of funerals. In fact, some who were there that day had been present when her husband died. They remember that she was younger then, not as gray as she is today. They recall her young, strong son, the spitting image of his dad, standing next to her. His loving concern for his mom is evident. Those who attended felt confident that this young man would step up and take care of his mom, now a widow. He had inherited the family property and livestock, and he would keep his father's business running. This means the woman would be cared for in her old age. But now, things have changed. Since her son died, she is not legally allowed to own the family business. Any other family assets will be sold out from under her to the highest bidder. In some cases, a flat-out swindle might occur as the unscrupulous prey upon this vulnerable and grieving woman. Jesus talked about those who would take advantage of defenseless widows in Luke 20:46-47 ESV: ***"Beware of the scribes, who like to walk around in long robes, and*** *love greetings in the marketplaces and the best seats in the synagogues and the places of honor at feasts, <u>who devour widows' houses and for a pretense make long prayers. They will receive the greater condemnation.</u>"*

This poor woman is defenseless against those swindlers who would exploit her situation, leaving her with hardly anything. If some kind soul doesn't take her in, she could end up homeless. Because of this, an atmosphere of distress hangs over the funeral procession. Unlike the crowd approaching the city, which is filled with joyful excitement, the crowd leaving the city feels the weight of grief and desperation tied to the woman's situation. Just then, something happens in Luke 7:13: **When the Lord saw her...**

As Jesus looked at this widow/mother, maybe He saw flashes of His past in this event. Did Christ think about his teenage mother giving birth in a stable? Or how upset Mary was when He stayed behind at the temple in Jerusalem? Did Jesus remember how He stepped up to help His mother Mary when Joseph passed?

Christ may have cringed at the thought of how His mother witnessed His horrible death. Did Jesus consider these things when He saw this poor, grieving woman? Perhaps. One thing we do know is that as Jesus sees this woman, He is emotionally touched. It says, **His heart went out to her.** When the Savior looks at her, He sees the pain that engulfs the world due to devastating loss. Jesus observes the grief that gnaws away at the human spirit whenever death comes calling. Christ recognizes the heartbreak a parent feels when burying their child. Jesus shares the same empathy that the Good Samaritan feels when he sees the beaten, robbed, and dying man lying in the ditch. The Savior takes pity on this grieving, hurting woman, just as the Father did when He was filled with compassion upon seeing His ragged and broken Prodigal son hobbling home. In that moment, Christ is awash with sympathy, compelling Him to intervene. Keep in mind that Jesus' encounter with the widow of Nain wasn't coincidental. He left for this out-of-the-way place long before the funeral procession began. The Savior climbs uphill on that narrow, dusty road, driven by the desire to mend this woman's broken heart.

Christ arrives at the right place at the right time so He can meet this despairing woman in her moment of great need. Likewise, the Lord Jesus Christ sees you in your moment of great need. When you sit in a hospital emergency room or stand at the graveside during one of the darkest moments of your life, Jesus is there. The Savior hears you when you cry those quiet tears in the middle of the night. Jesus sees you when anxiety sets in or when sickness grabs hold of you. When fear attacks, when pain assaults, when the darkness of depression engulfs you, or when you're caught in the floodwaters of loneliness, Jesus sees you, and He comes to heal your hurting heart. Jesus not only knows when these things occur; He does something about them. Yes, the Great Physician attends to all our ailments. Nothing is beyond the reach of His loving touch. His power conquers all, heals all, and pulls us out of the deepest pit life digs for us.

Nothing can stand in His way. Nothing can break His loving grip. Nothing is impossible for Him. The grieving woman doesn't know that God knows, but He does. In this moment, she doesn't think that God cares, but He does. For this reason, Jesus came. Can you see Jesus walking over to the grieving mother? She has a confused look on her face because she doesn't know who He is or what He wants. I can imagine Christ putting His hand on the woman's shoulder, then leaning in to say, ***"Don't cry."*** But is this a valid request?

Is it right to ask a grieving parent not to cry after losing her only son? It doesn't seem fair, does it? Truthfully, only Jesus has the right to say, ***"Don't cry,"*** because Jesus is the answer to every problem, heartache, and struggle we face. In this instance, it's not just what Jesus says that matters; it's what Christ implies: Don't cry, I'm here.

Also, don't overlook how easily Christ transitions from one crowd to another. First, the Savior is in the midst of the crowd filled with joyful expectation. Next, He slides alongside the crowd, steeped in sorrow. The lesson here is clear: Jesus meets us wherever we are, giving us whatever we need. The Savior stands with us in our happiness, while also holding us up when things seem hopeless.

***Then He went up and touched the bier, and those carrying it stood still.*** Verse 14 In doing this, Jesus caught everyone off guard. The Savior didn't just touch the stretcher holding the deceased; the 1st Century burial practice didn't include a wooden box or coffin; rather, the body was wrapped in a typical burial cloth. Jesus laid His hand on the young man's body. Some of the crowd shivered since, according to the Law, Jesus had rendered Himself 'unclean' by touching the dead. BUT, let's hit the pause button for a moment. There's someone else present on this day. Someone unseen was walking among this company of mourners. This unseen person isn't grieving; he's celebrating this moment of human heartbreak.

He's feasting on the sorrow and drinking in the misery of this event. This unseen person is the devil himself. How do I know this is true? I believe that wherever Jesus' ministry takes Him, Satan is one step behind. If anyone kept his friends close and his enemies closer, it was Lucifer. So, imagine what happens when the King of Kings steps forward; the devil panics and flees. When the Light of the World puts His hand on that dead body, the darkness flickers and then fades. When the Son of the Most High God puts His hand on the body of that young man, Heaven smiles as death dies. ***"Young man, I say to you, get up!"*** (verse 14).

It started slowly, with the twitch of a hand or a subtle movement of a leg. The pallbearers notice the stirring and begin to panic. They want to drop the litter and run, but they don't. Before they can react, ***the dead man sits up and starts to talk.*** I wonder what he said once the funeral shroud fell away from his face? I think he might have said, "Where's my mom?" She's right there, in shock and confusion, seeing her dead son alive, sitting up and talking. She might have stood there in frozen disbelief for who knows how long if Jesus hadn't intervened. It says, verse 15…***and Jesus gave him back to his mother.*** Imagine: all the promises the young man made, all the protection and provision he was giving his mother, all his best intentions came back to life with him. This miraculous reversal from dead to alive creates a cosmic shockwave that rattles the gates of hell.

Pardon the interruption, Mr. Dark Prince. You see, the true Prince of Peace is now in control. Satan, you are dismissed. Your kingdom is crumbling. Your dominion is disintegrating. Your chokehold on humanity is losing its grip. Why? Because the Son of God has come to defeat sin, death, and you, too, Father of Lies. 1 John 3:8 tells us, ***The reason the Son of Man appeared was to destroy the devil's work.*** This means that Jesus, the Lion of Judah, is on a search-and-destroy mission, so this is a taste of what's to come, Beelzebub, and you know it.

The final knockout blow will occur at Calvary, confirmed by Colossians 2:15, ***And having disarmed the powers and authorities, He made a public spectacle of them, triumphing over them by the cross.***

It's as if Paul suggests that Christ, after He died on the cross, parades the Adversary of God and all his evil cohorts behind Him like a conquering King. Since then, the Great Serpent is back where he belongs, once again on his belly. Can you hear that crunching sound predicted in Genesis 3:15? ***"...and He will crush your head, and you will strike at his heel."***

August 4, 2023, marked seven years since my wife died of cancer. We were married for over 40 years. Not a day goes by that I don't think about her. There are many days when I long to be with her. If there's anything I've learned, it's that grief isn't the enemy. Loss is the real villain. Grief is normal and necessary; it's the emotional mechanism God provides to help us process loss.

Over time, grief subsides, but loss remains. Loss is that hole in your life where the person you love once stood. Gradually, over many weeks, months, and even years, you learn how to navigate around that hole. But someday, there will be no hole. We will be reunited with our loved ones in glory, forever. What will that look like? Revelation 21:4 (ESV) gives us the answer. ***"He will wipe away every tear from their eyes, and death shall be no more, neither shall there be mourning, nor crying, nor pain anymore, for the former things have passed away."***

So, until that time or the next time you find yourself backed into a corner, especially when you feel the cruel circumstances of life crashing down on you, don't give up. Don't give in. Do look up, expecting Jesus to say, "Don't cry, because I never left, and I never will." Someday, we'll all be together again. Come, Lord Jesus.

## Chapter 3 Questions

1. What does this reveal about Jesus, who travels to such an out-of-the-way place like Nain? How has the Lord shown up unexpectedly for you?

2. What emotions have you experienced at funerals you have attended throughout your life?

3. How do you believe our society handles the experiences of grief and loss?

4. What are some supportive ways to help someone who is grieving?

5. Imagine the root cause of the emotions Jesus felt as He looked at that funeral procession.

6. Do you believe that Christ's encounter with the widow was accidental or intentional? Have you ever felt that Jesus didn't show up during your hour of crisis?

7. Imagine that you are a pallbearer at this funeral. What thoughts might cross your mind as the deceased shows signs of life?

8. Imagine and describe the reunion in Heaven when we reunite with our loved ones.

# The Transfiguration

## Luke 9:28-36

*About eight days after Jesus said this, He took Peter, John, and James with Him and went up onto a mountain to pray. As He was praying, the appearance of His face changed, and His clothes became as bright as a flash of lightning. Two men, Moses and Elijah, appeared in glorious splendor, talking with Jesus. They spoke about His departure, which He was about to bring to fulfillment at Jerusalem.*

*Peter and his companions were very sleepy, but when they became fully awake, they saw His glory and the two men standing with Him. As the men were leaving Jesus, Peter said to Him, "Master, it is good for us to be here. Let us put up three shelters—one for You, one for Moses, and one for Elijah." (He did not know what he was saying.)*

*While he was speaking, a cloud appeared and covered them, and they were afraid as they entered the cloud. A voice came from the cloud, saying, "This is My Son, whom I have chosen; listen to Him." When the voice had spoken, they found that Jesus was alone. The disciples kept this to themselves and did not tell anyone at that time what they had seen.*

Luke 9:28-36

IF YOU WANT TO TALK ABOUT A MOUNTAINTOP EXPERIENCE, this is it. Peter, James, and John have no idea what the day will bring until Jesus pulls them aside. Suddenly, they find themselves standing with Christ at the base of Mt. Tabor. Maybe the Savior just said, 'Follow Me' and then started climbing. Maybe He didn't say anything before beginning His ascent. Bewildered, Peter, James, and John watch Jesus scale the vertical cliff. So, as Jesus continues to climb, these three disciples join Him.

From the very beginning, it's tough going. Leather sandals don't offer much traction on slippery flat rocks and sliding dirt. These three men likely resembled first-timers on ice skates. Their sea legs enable them to stand comfortably in any boat, climbing over and dropping down the rolling waves. They're accustomed to the sun in their eyes and the wind on their faces, with an occasional sea spray washing over them. However, mountain climbing is vastly different from being out on the open sea. Scurrying up the steep side of a mountain is as unfamiliar to them as walking on the moon. Yet, despite their stumbling and lack of experience, they continue to climb. Mt. Tabor is not just a swollen hill; it's a small mountain standing about 2,000 feet tall. Perhaps you can relate. You might be facing a mountain right now. What started as a simple hike has turned into a steady uphill ascent. Your job is becoming more challenging. Your bank account is dwindling. Your health is declining. Hope for a bright future is fading into the twilight of uncertainty. This isn't what you signed up for.

Just like the three disciples, you're headed where you don't want to go. Remember, wherever God leads us is the best place we can be. However, that doesn't mean the journey will be easy. Please don't forget that the Savior is climbing alongside you. Imagine Peter, James, and John, red-faced and huffing and puffing, grunting and reaching for the next handhold. These disciples are out of their element as loose dirt and rocks slide away from beneath their feet. Looking at one another in disbelief, they wonder how far and high they will be climbing.

Remember, these men are sailors, not mountain goats. I can picture Jesus looking back over His shoulder, smiling as they follow His lead. Isn't that what the Christian faith is all about? Jesus leads; we follow. He picks the path, sets the pace, and shows us the way. We follow behind Him, determined to stay close. This is a biblical strategy according to

1 John 2:6 ESV, ***Whoever says he abides in Him ought to walk in the same way in which He walked.*** We step in Christ's footprints, mimicking His movements and striving to go in the same direction. Did you know that when I walk, my right foot turns out slightly, just like my father's? One time, as I was walking toward someone, she remarked, "I know who you are. I can tell by the way you walk. You walk just like your father."

Do people know who your Heavenly Father is by the way you walk? Can they see the nature of God's love reflected in your actions?

Eventually, Jesus reaches His desired destination to pray. He wants to put distance between Himself and the crowds, hoping for some privacy. But why take Peter, James, and John with Him? Why push them to these heights, making them sweaty, dirty, and tired? There is a specific reason. Luke 9:29 tells us, *And as He was praying, the appearance of His face changed, and His clothes became as bright as a flash of lightning.*

This begs the question: Did this transformation occur in Jesus from another source, from the outside in, or did this transfiguration originate from Jesus Himself, from the inside out?

Well, this dramatic and glorious change came from Jesus Himself. In that moment, the Son of God pulls back the curtain on His humanity, revealing the glory and splendor of His divinity. This was more than breathtaking; it was overwhelming. We're told that His clothes became as *bright as a flash of lightning*.

Now, lightning is something we stare at when it flashes in the distance. But up close, lightning is frightening, as experienced by Mr. Ross Sullivan. Mr. Sullivan served as a park ranger at Shenandoah National Park in Virginia for almost 30 years. Due to his experiences, Park Ranger Sullivan is listed in the Guinness Book of World Records under the title, "Most Lightning Strikes Survived." Park Ranger Sullivan was struck by lightning seven times, earning him the nickname "Spark Ranger."

Did you know that a bolt of lightning is as bright as one million 100-watt light bulbs? The heat generated by a lightning bolt can be five times hotter than the surface of the sun, reaching temperatures of 50,000 degrees. Why did Jesus need these special effects? What is the Savior trying to convey to his three weary disciples? Then again, if this scene of Jesus' Transfiguration isn't spectacular enough, what happens next staggers the human imagination. Suddenly, two Old Testament superheroes show up: Moses and Elijah.

When they walked this earth, each had a mountaintop experience with God. Both had an unusual departure from this world. Moses died, but the Lord God buried him; to this day, no one knows where. Elijah receives a first-class seat on a fiery chariot taking him to Heaven while still alive. Some conclude that Moses represents the Law and Elijah the prophets. These two men are plucked from Heaven to step into the spotlight of Christ's glory and have a conversation with Him. Meanwhile, Peter, James, and John are listening in. What do they hear? Well, they hear about Christ's departure (His death), which was about to be fulfilled in Jerusalem. Moses, Elijah, and Jesus talked about Christ's purpose in coming to earth, His sacrificial death, and resurrection that would bring salvation to the world—pretty important stuff.

Keep in mind that we are still uncertain why Jesus wanted His three disciples to witness this dramatic, supernatural demonstration of His Deity, alongside the presence of two Old Testament heroes. What was the point? Did you know that Christ mentions His resurrection twenty-one times in the Gospels? He repeatedly tells His disciples how things will play out. One would think they were on board. If you look at Luke 9:20-22, Jesus turns to His disciples, asking this important question in verse 9:20: *"Who do you say that I am?" Peter answered, "God's Messiah."* Verse 22 *And He* [Jesus] *said, "The Son of Man must suffer many things and be rejected by the elders, the chief priests, and the teachers of the law, and He must be killed, and on the third day be raised to life."*

Now it seems that everyone, especially Peter, understands. But isn't this the same Peter who, when Christ talks about what is going to happen, the big fisherman soundly rejects it in Matthew 16:21-23, *From that time on, Jesus began to explain to His disciples that He must go to Jerusalem and suffer many things at the hands of the elders, the chief priests, and the teachers of the law, and that He must be killed and on the third day be raised to life. Peter took Him aside and began to rebuke Him. "Never, Lord!" he said. "This shall never happen to you!" Jesus turned and said to Peter, "Get behind Me, Satan! You are a stumbling block to Me; you do not have in mind the concerns of God, but merely human concerns."*

Peter didn't have his sights set on what God wanted. He was fixated on what the disciples expected to happen. They failed to realize the true mission and purpose of Christ's coming. Nevertheless, Heaven's timeline was progressing, and the clock was ticking. The transfiguration was a wake-up call for the disciples to accept the reality of Christ's mission.

Unfortunately, the disciples had their own narrative regarding God's salvation plan. They believed that Jesus would enter Jerusalem as a conquering hero, and they would ride in on His coattails. Then, Jesus would drive out the Romans and restore the city to the Jews, making the disciples big shots. Nothing could be further from the truth. Simon Peter is one of my favorite Bible characters because he's passionately spontaneous, a swing-first, ask-questions-later kind of guy, who suffers from an acute case of foot-in-mouth disease. This becomes obvious in Luke 9:33, *As the men were leaving Jesus, Peter said to Him, "Master it is good for us to be here.*

**Let us put up three shelters- one for you, one for Moses, and one for Elijah." (He did not know what he was saying.)**

I've wondered how Peter knew it was Moses and Elijah. Doubtfully, they were wearing name tags. Did Jesus make some formal introduction? If you have the answer, I'd love to hear it. Do you realize what Peter is doing? This is the first-century version of a 'Midwestern good-bye.' If you live in the Midwest, you've experienced it; you may have done it. You are guests at someone's house, and you announce that it's time to leave. They're disappointed, asking if they can interest you in some warmed-up tater-tot hot dish. "No thanks, the meal was great, and we really must get going." So, you stand up, they stand up, and you look at each other until you say, "Can we have our coats?" "Oh, Bill, get their coats." Next come goodbyes and hugs. Now you're moving toward the door, but your hosts are right with you.

As you walk to your car, your hosts follow, prompting another conversation, followed by another round of goodbyes and more hugs. Finally, you get in the car and begin to back out. Your hosts walk to the edge of the driveway, almost standing in the street. You wave one last time as they frantically wave back like they're stranded on a desert island, watching you drive off. That's a Midwestern goodbye. But why was Peter stalling? I must admit, I would love to visit with Jesus, Moses, and Elijah as well. I'd enjoy spending some time with them, drinking coffee and discussing the Exodus and Elijah's issues with Jezebel. But Peter's attempt to delay it goes deeper.

I believe that the disciples, especially Peter, had no concept of the Divine timeline that was already set in motion. They were unaware of how soon things would unfold. Therefore, they needed a dramatic wake-up call. Enter the cloud with a thunderous voice from Heaven.

You know, there was another time when God the Father delivered a specific message. It's at Christ's baptism in Matthew 3:16-17, *As soon as Jesus was baptized, He went up out of the water. At that moment, Heaven was opened, and He saw the Spirit of God descending like a dove, and alighting on Him. And a voice from Heaven said, "This is My Son, whom I love; with Him I am well pleased."*

This is a message of affirmation from the Father to His Son. Right after this, Jesus begins His earthly ministry. The next stop is the wilderness, where Jesus locks horns with the devil for 40 days. So, what God the Father is saying to Jesus is, "I'm with you. You got this!"

However, the second message is directed to a different audience. It's not for Jesus, but for His disciples. Luke 9:34-35, *While he* [Peter] *was speaking, a cloud appeared and covered them, and they were afraid as they entered the cloud. A voice from the cloud, saying, "This is My Son, whom I have chosen, listen to Him."* This message was for the disciples who weren't listening to Christ. They missed the plain and simple explanations about what was about to happen. Jesus told them flat out. Their lack of understanding prompts the Savior to resort to this dramatic show-and-tell by giving His disciples a glimpse of His divinity on that mountaintop, accompanied by special appearances from Moses and Elijah. It is capped off by God the Father's verbal instruction for the disciples to pay attention and listen.

All too often, we are busy trying to set the agenda for God, rather than following God's leading. Psalm 37:4 ESV is the kind of verse most people like to quote. It mentions that the Lord God **will give you the desires of your heart.** Can there be better news than this? This suggests that the Lord is a kind of celestial Santa Claus, ready to grant us anything we desire. However, the first part of the verse casts a different light on the whole verse: **Delight yourself in the Lord, and He will give you the desires of your heart.** Well, if you love God, then delighting yourself in Him is no big deal, right? However, delighting yourself in the Lord means wanting what the Lord wants. It means our desires must align with God's heart. Therefore, if we desire what the Lord wants for us, God will give us the desires of our heart. Let's take this a step further: what if the thing we want is not what the Lord wants for us? This means that when we pray, **"Your will be done, on earth as it is in Heaven"** (Matthew 6:10 ESV).

We should be willing to accept God's will, even when we don't like it or want it. We should always examine the desires of our hearts by asking this question: "What if God doesn't want me to have what I want?" In simple terms, we must want what God wants. Confusion persists and frustration abounds when we try to impose our narrative into God's story. That's what the disciples continued to do throughout their three years with Jesus.

Then, when Christ is arrested, Peter denies the Savior three times. In Peter's mind, this was not supposed to happen, so he couldn't handle this outcome. When Christ dies, the disciples are thrown into a panic. They hide in the upper room, locking the door and pulling the shades while cowering in fear. Every time they hear a noise outside, they shake with terror, thinking the Romans are coming for them. The Savior tried to spare them from this, but they weren't listening. They ignored God the Father's instruction to pay attention to what Jesus is telling them. Sometimes our frustration occurs because we aren't tuned into the Lord, who speaks to us in the quietness of our heart, through His word, and through other believers. Just like the disciples, we stumble and fall until the Lord picks us up. We tend to do the wrong thing or say the wrong thing to God and others, but the Lord never gives up on us.

We often misunderstand and misrepresent God. However, the Lord continues to work on changing us. As followers of Christ, we are always in the process of transformation, for He who began a good work in us will complete it. The Lord does not view us for who we are or what we have done; God sees us for who we can become. We are constantly in a state of 'becoming' since Jesus is the author and finisher of our faith. Through the Lord's mercy and grace, we are becoming better men and women, better husbands and wives, better grandparents, better sons and daughters, better neighbors, better friends, and better people overall. It doesn't matter how the world perceives us; what matters is how we act on what we know.

We know that Jesus saves and Jesus stays, bringing life-changing power when He does. I'm sure you have heard about the Asbury Revival that took place in February 2023 at Asbury University in Kentucky. It lasted for two weeks, with students and visitors from around the country and the world attending. It was 24 hours of non-stop worship, praise, and prayer, accompanied by the glorious outpouring of the Holy Spirit. Testimonies were shared, lives were transformed, and healings took place. Many have tried to explain or understand it, but I have a simplistic view about it. The Lord God can do whatever He wants, wherever He wants, whenever He wants to do it. He doesn't need our permission or understanding. This often occurs in the lives of inmates in the jail where I work.

This past week, a man named Marcus sent me a message, as inmates can email departments like the Commissary, Medical, Food Service, or the Chaplain. Marcus' message to me was just one question: "What does redemption mean?" I wrote back explaining redemption, but I also asked, "Marcus, have you experienced redemption? Is this something you want to talk about?" Within hours, Marcus wrote back in all caps, "YES CHAPLAIN, I NEED TO TALK TO YOU ABOUT THIS."

When I met Marcus, he was nervous and reluctant to speak. After making small talk, he said he had a story to tell me. "The other night, I was in my cell, locked in for the night. The lights were off, and I was lying in my bunk. I did something I haven't done in years. I began to pray. As I lay there praying, I heard a voice saying only one word: 'Redemption.' This is why I asked you what it meant." Marcus and I talked about redemption, which provided me the opportunity to share the Gospel message. Marcus' heart was open, so he prayed for Jesus to become his Savior and Lord. There are two reasons why this happened. The Lord God can do whatever He wants, wherever He wants, whenever He wants to do it. The second reason is that Marcus was listening. Are you listening?

## Chapter 4 Questions

1. Can you think of a time when God led you into a difficult circumstance, a place where you didn't want to be? What did God teach you through that experience?

2. In what ways can someone demonstrate their willingness to follow God's leading?

3. Why were the disciples struggling to accept the ultimate purpose and mission of Jesus?

4. After studying Psalm 37:4, what new insights have you gained? How does this compare to your previous understanding of this verse?

5. Why do our preconceived notions about what we need often conflict with God's view of what's best for us?

6. What habits or tendencies often stand in the way of hearing God's voice? How can someone overcome these hindrances to perceive what the Lord wants us to do?

7. Have you set aside time each day for daily Bible reading and prayer?

8. How much of that prayer time is spent listening instead of asking?

# The Adulterous Woman

## John 8:2-11

*At dawn He (Jesus) appeared again in the temple courts, where all the people gathered around Him, and He sat down to teach them. The teachers of the law and the Pharisees brought in a woman caught in adultery. They made her stand before the group and said to Jesus, "Teacher, this woman was caught in the act of adultery. In the Law, Moses commanded us to stone such women. Now what do you say?" They were using this question as a trap in order to have a basis for accusing Him.*

*But Jesus bent down and started to write on the ground with His finger. When they kept on questioning Him, He straightened up and said to them, "Let any one of you who is without sin be the first to throw a stone at her." Again He stooped down and wrote on the ground.*

*At this, those who heard began to go away one at a time, the older ones first, until only Jesus was left, with the woman still standing there. Jesus straightened up and asked her, "Woman, where are they? Has no one condemned you?" "No one, sir," she said. "Then neither do I condemn you," Jesus declared. "Go now and leave your life of sin."*

John 8:2-11

THIS IS NO CINDERELLA STORY. There will be no palace ball, with a glass slipper left behind—no gallant rescue by some handsome prince. The men in this story are anything but royal and far from charming. They view this woman as someone to be used and discarded, a throwaway kind of person. The woman in this story is someone we all know, or someone we know of. Think back to your pre-teen years to the girl who matured early. This sudden change was much envied by her female friends but delighted the boys in her class. She was often the topic of conversation as the boys huddled on the playground. With all this newfound popularity, this young girl began to confuse attention for affection, eventually mistaking lust for love. She fell prey to the false notion that men liked her when they just wanted to have her. It seemed like she came with instructions that read, "Take what you want, as much as you need, and leave when you've had your fill." This painful pattern repeated countless times until her life became a series of bad relationships. Nevertheless, her quest for love drove her to keep trying.

One day, a handsome young man who never paid much attention to her suddenly appeared to be more than a little interested. However, his attraction had a sinister purpose, orchestrated by others who knew the girl was easily lured into compromising situations with men. We don't know if this meeting was spontaneous or pre-planned.

Nevertheless, this young woman had no idea that the invitation was part of a bigger plan. It seems those who engineered this meeting intended to use it to trap Jesus in a moral dilemma. This evil scheme allowed the planners to wait for just the right moment to barge in and catch this couple (verse 4) ***"...in the act of adultery."*** How could they do this unless they were lying in wait? Imagine the embarrassment she feels as they yank her from the bed. But to her surprise, her male counterpart just lies there smiling.

The Scribes and Pharisees toss him a small pouch filled with a few coins, which he catches in mid-air. As he shakes the pouch and begins to count his reward, they drag her out of the house. Even as this woman looks back in desperation, the man never looks up. That's when the nightmare begins.

Very quickly, her confusion turns to shame as they pull and shove her down the streets. Along the way, she's subjected to more abuse in the form of harsh language, deepening her humiliation. She's too frightened to ask where they're taking her, but when they begin to climb the temple steps, she starts to tremble. She falls multiple times, tripped up by fear and apprehension, which leads to more rough handling by the small mob controlling her fate. Once inside the temple, she stumbles again; that's when she looks up to see a crowd in the corner of the temple court, but they hardly notice her. They're busy listening to someone sitting on a wall, teaching them.

Afraid of public humiliation, she hesitates, only to be scooped up by the rough hands of her accusers, who drag her the rest of the way. Without stopping, the mob hauling the young woman pushes through the crowd. A few bystanders protest but quickly grow quiet when they see the Pharisees leading the way. They shove the woman one more time, causing her to fall hard onto the stone floor with a loud slap. She finds herself at the feet of the Teacher, yet she dares not make eye contact. As the woman lies there, she feels the penetrating glare of the crowd. Just then, one of the Pharisees speaks to the man sitting on the wall. But not before this lead Pharisee grabs the woman by the hair, forcing her to stand. Still, her eyes look down in shame and fear. This Pharisee speaks with bitterness as he points toward her with contempt. *"Teacher, this woman was caught in the act of adultery. In the Law, Moses commanded us to stone such women. Now what do You say?"* (John 8:4-5)

That's when the woman realizes what they're up to. Now she understands that her life could end beneath a barrage of rocks hurled by an angry crowd. She continues to tremble under this threat. Her mind revisits the scene with her bedmate and stops when she looks over to see him smiling and shaking the coins out of the pouch. That's when she comprehends this was a setup. This accusing Pharisee addressing Jesus knows the Law all too well, which is why he doesn't quote it word for word. In Leviticus 20:10, it says, *"If a man commits adultery with another man's wife--with the wife of his neighbor— both the adulterer and the adulteress are to be put to death."*

Then in Deuteronomy 22:22 ESV we read: *"If a man is found lying with the wife of another man, both of them shall die, the man who lay with the woman and the woman. So you must purge the evil from Israel."* So, where's the guy who's equally guilty? How come he gets a free pass? Why isn't he threatened with death by stoning? We can guess why: because the whole situation is a set-up, with the real target of this scheme being Jesus Himself. We might refer to this as a trap within a trap. Meanwhile, the crowd is fired up by the Pharisee's accusation of the woman. So, all eyes are on Jesus, wondering what He will do or say. But Jesus remains silent at first. Instead, He kneels and begins to write on the ground with His finger.

If Jesus says, "stone her," He violates Roman law, which forbids anyone except a Roman court from sentencing someone to death. If Jesus says, "Don't stone her," He could be accused of defying the Law of Moses. This situation is referred to as a 'double bind.' However, let's take a moment to examine the crowd. As we do, we realize that on any given day, each of us stands in a crowd of people just like this. Each of us carries a handful of stones. This means that if we pass judgment on someone, we throw a stone. If we refuse to forgive someone, we throw a stone. If we ridicule or reject anyone, we throw a stone.

Whenever we consider someone less important than us or more sinful than we are, we throw a stone. Whenever we despise someone because of their politics, skin color, or choices, we throw a stone. Yes, all of us are accomplished stone-throwers. We have honed our aim and strengthened our tendency to fire, launch, fling, and hurl our opinions, judgments, and condemnations at anyone we don't like. This means that stone-throwing is never accidental; it's always intentional. Stone-throwing isn't a misguided, spontaneous reaction. It is always a deliberate assault on someone's reputation, lifestyle, or personal beliefs. Sadly, we are as quick to punish as we are to judge.

Now, as the tension builds due to Jesus' silence, the accusers of this woman demand a response. Jesus straightens up to make a statement, addressing the entire crowd and us here today. He says in John 8:7-9, ***"Let any one of you who is without sin be the first to throw a stone at her." Again, He*** *stooped down and wrote on the ground. At this, those who heard began to go away, one at a time, the older ones first, until only Jesus was left, with the woman still standing there.*

We stand in that crowd, rocks in hand, as a voice calls out to us, forcing us to look deep within ourselves. This voice belongs to Jesus, who says, *"Let any one of you who is without sin be the first to throw a stone at her."*

Slowly, the crowd begins to thin out, with the older men leaving first. They know themselves all too well, familiar with the darkness that hides within them. So do we, as the rock we hold becomes heavy with conviction. The stone we've chosen cuts us deeply, revealing the truth about ourselves.

Let anyone who has not lied, lusted, criticized, or despised someone throw the first stone. Let that perfect person choose their target and let their rocks of intolerance fly. Ready! Aim! WAIT!

Wouldn't it be better if we simply dropped the rock we're holding, since we have no right to throw stones? Why not let go of our hatred, unforgiveness, and hasty judgments, along with the contempt we hold against anyone for anything? Why not release our prejudice, misguided assumptions, and our tendency to dislike or diminish others? Drop your rock unless you're perfect. Take aim only if you have never missed the mark yourself. Fire away if you have always been on target with your thoughts, words, and actions.

When I was pastoring in New York State, my family lived in a parsonage on the church property. My kids would often visit me. One time, they showed up with what they called a "neat rock." It was flat and round, and they decided it would be a good gift for me. Unsure of what to do with it, I left it on my desk. Then, I thought of this story. I took out a bottle of 'white-out.' Remember white-out? I used the white-out to write on the rock, "The First Stone," and then I placed it in my desk drawer. When someone came to my office to complain about someone else, I would reach into my drawer, pull out the stone, and place it on the edge of my desk with the letters facing down. Then, I would tell them to pick it up and read it. Whenever someone read the words "The First Stone," they would become quiet. Then they would gently set the rock down on my desk. Eventually, they would get up and leave because nothing more needed to be said.

Do you have any rocks you need to set down? Just think about the fact that **all have sinned and fall short of the glory of God.** (Romans 3:23) We are all broken, every one of us. We live in a broken world. All of us need the help and support of those around us. Isn't it time we drop our fistful of rocks and start building each other up instead of tearing each other down? Drop your rock so your hands can be ready to lift the fallen.

Let go, so you can restore the broken and help heal the hurting. But approach it differently this time. Remember how lost you were before you were saved. Admit how often you stumble, even now, instead of walking by faith. Acknowledge that you need God's loving forgiveness as much as anyone else. God's word tells us clearly, **While we were still sinners, Christ died for us.** (Romans 5:8) Before we deserved forgiveness, the Lord made it available. Why? John 3:17 gives us the answer: **"For God did not send His Son into the world to condemn the world, but to save the world through Him."**

So, then, drop your stones and get on your knees, assuming the posture of a beggar, telling another beggar where to find bread. Isn't that what the Gospel message really is? Stop being a stone-thrower and become a message bearer instead. Along the way, don't expect the lost to behave like they're saved. Understand that non-Christians can't act like Christians if they don't know Christ. Remember that even though we have Jesus, how often do we act as if we don't?

The problem with the world isn't the other people in it; the real issue is sin, which affects all people. Sin is the tool evil uses to infect our world. We need to stop acting as if our neighbor or even some stranger is the problem. Here's why, *For we do not wrestle against flesh and blood, but against the rulers, against the authorities, against the cosmic powers over this present darkness, against the spiritual forces of evil in heavenly places* (Ephesians 6:12).

Recognize that we are ensnared by evil in this world. Some people believe that a jail is an evil place. Yet, when I speak to inmates, I don't see evil in their eyes. I see souls adrift in a sea of hopelessness. I see individuals striving to find their way out of the darkness. That's why Jesus described His ministry this way in Luke 4:18 NLT: *"The Spirit of the LORD is upon Me, for He has anointed Me to bring Good News to the poor. He has sent Me to proclaim that captives will be released, that the blind will see, that the oppressed will be set free."*

Never forget that evil is relentless. Evil seeks to trip us up, hoping to knock us down and keep us there. It is always prepared to fill our hands with more rocks, pushing us to target anyone we dislike or who might be different. The more rocks we carry in our arsenal, the greater our tendency to throw one. So, why not let go of the stones you're holding?

Begin today to live differently by giving grace willingly. *Everyone should be quick to listen, slow to speak and slow to become angry* (James 1:19). Remember, if you're saved, the Lord has spared you from His judgment, so why not spare others from yours? *Be kind and compassionate to one another, forgiving each other, just as in Christ God forgave you* (Ephesians 4:32).

Well, it's time for Jesus to stand up and speak to the woman in front of Him. Her head is still down because she's drenched in shame and fearful of accusation. Guess what? We're standing there with her. However, our sins are usually more private than hers. Still, we realize that if people knew what we sometimes do or think, we would fall prey to the rocks of rejection, just like this woman. We would be crushed beneath the stones of no second chances. So, like this woman, we hold our breath, waiting to see what God will do.

First, Jesus straightens up and brushes off His hands. Then He looks at this woman and us and says (John 8:10-11): *"Where are they? Has no one condemned you?" "No one, Sir," she said. "Then neither do I condemn you."* That's when we breathe a collective sigh of relief. *Therefore, there is now no condemnation for those who are in Christ Jesus* (Romans 8:1). Remember, the Lord God didn't save us because we're perfect; God saves us because we're not, and we will never be perfect in this life. Therefore, we need to stop holding ourselves and others to impossible standards of perfection. We should start giving ourselves and others more grace, more love, and more forgiveness because that's what the Lord gives us.

But don't stop there; consider the last thing Jesus says to the woman: ***"Go now and leave your life of sin"*** (John 8:11).

Just don't wish you could be a better person; *be* a better person.

*You have the tools*; you *know* the changes you should make. If you don't know how or feel stuck in patterns and habits you can't break, follow King David's example in Psalm 139:22-24 NLT by praying this prayer: ***Search me, O God, and know my heart; test me and know my anxious thoughts. Point out anything in me that offends you and lead me along the path of everlasting life.***

Ask the Lord to help you see if you have a judgmental, prejudicial, or critical spirit. The first step in this process of self-discovery is to acknowledge that we all throw stones. So, why not drop the stones you're carrying *here* and *now*? Step away from the tendency to ridicule those who think or live differently from you. Let go of the stones you're holding. Release them now.

Stop viewing people as a threat simply because they're different. Start seeing people the way the Lord God does: either they *know* the Truth, or they *need* the Truth. This Truth isn't merely a concept or a belief; it is a person, and that person is Jesus Christ, who said, ***"I am the way, the truth, and the life, no comes to the Father except through Me"*** (John 14:6). Those of us who know the Truth must live out that truth because we can't be the hands and feet of Jesus unless we have the Heart of Jesus. This is only possible when we stop throwing stones.

## Chapter 5 Questions

1.  If we understand that making snap judgments about others is hurtful, why do we keep doing it?

2.  If you were there and heard Jesus say, ***"If anyone is without sin, let him throw the first stone,"*** what might you be thinking?

3.  If you pray the prayer that David prays in Psalm 139:23-24 NLT: ***Search me, O God, and know my heart; test me and know my anxious thoughts. Point out anything in me that offends you, and lead me along the path of everlasting life.*** What might happen?

4.  Sometimes the heaviest rock we carry is unforgiveness. Is there someone you need to forgive?

5. When we look at someone, we quickly identify the sin behind that person. What's the reasoning behind their sin? Does this insight help us be more understanding?

6. Scottish writer Ian MacLaren wrote, "Be kind, for everyone you meet is fighting a hard battle you know nothing about." Do you agree? Or is this just an excuse for their behavior?

7. Imagine being the woman in this story. How would you feel when Jesus said, *"Neither do I condemn you"* (John 8:11). Have you ever experienced this kind of Divine forgiveness?

8. What was behind Jesus' parting comment to the woman: *"Go now and leave your life of sin"?* (John 8:11)

# The Ten Lepers

## Luke 17:11-19

*Now on His way to Jerusalem, Jesus traveled along the border between Samaria and Galilee. As He was going into a village, ten men who had leprosy met Him. They stood at a distance and called out in a loud voice, "Jesus, Master, have pity on us!"*

*When He saw them, He said, "Go, show yourselves to the priests." And as they went, they were cleansed.*

*One of them, when he saw he was healed, came back, praising God in a loud voice. He threw himself at Jesus' feet and thanked Him, and he was a Samaritan.*

*Jesus asked, "Were not all ten cleansed? Where are the other nine? Has no one returned to give praise to God except this foreigner?" Then He said to him, "Rise and go; your faith has made you well."*

Luke 17:11-19

TEN MEN ARE IN A PLACE WHERE NO ONE WANTS TO BE. It's a lonely space of painful isolation with no escape. It's a dreadful location, a no man's land, filled with sorrow and shame. Each man carries his own story of how he ended up there, a life once filled with pleasant memories from the distant past. These men lived like everyone else, never imagining they could lose everything. It never occurred to them that they would become outcasts of society, rejected and scorned, exiled to this desolate place of endless suffering.

By now, the people they love are long gone or, at least, keeping a safe distance. Their wives, along with the children they tucked into bed at night, have vanished. They've moved on because they had no choice; it was the safest thing to do. For this reason, these ten men rarely talk about their former lives; it's just too painful to remember.

One can only guess how these ten men came together. They found each other and formed a brotherhood of misery, stranded in this space of lonely despair. They created a fraternity of contamination that no one joins willingly. These ten men exist in this purgatory of endless suffering. They endure mangled limbs, deformed faces, and missing fingers and toes. Barely surviving, rarely moving around, as every step brings pain.

The hours between sunrise and sunset are filled with agonizing isolation, causing one bleak day to merge into the next due to this terrible disease. Frequently, they remain in this limbo between two countries, where two cultures clash and harbor mutual disdain. Here is where these ten men live. These ten men are lepers, and this is their story.

In verse 1, we're told that Jesus was traveling through this area on His way to Jerusalem. On His journey to confront the corrupt justice of Rome and face the religious elite, Jesus walks through this region, hugging the border between two countries. That's where He often goes, positioned in the midst of where He should be, in the middle of our pain, heartache, and confusion. Not standing back, but stepping in. He is engaging, participating, and pursuing us; wherever we are, He is always willing to provide what we need.

We're told in verse 12 that Jesus was heading into a village. We don't know why He was going there, but the Savior is always aware of His surroundings, always tuned into those people standing on the periphery of society: the lost souls with broken lives and the discarded ones often forgotten. However, this group of ten men is determined not to go unnoticed. They maintain a safe distance as required by law, wearing bells to signal a warning and calling out, "Unclean! Unclean!" if someone approaches. Just look at their tattered clothing and smell the stench of decay that's undeniable. The limping, hobbling, and clinging to each other for support is hard to miss. If that isn't enough, the tree branches used for crutches and canes give them away. But when this Jesus of Nazareth passes by, it's time for action. They've heard the stories about His miraculous healings. So, they call out to Him in a loud voice, ***"Jesus, Master, have pity on us!"*** (Luke 17:13).

This group not only knows who Christ is, but they also believe in what He can do for them. If this is true, why did they ask for pity instead of healing? Why not clearly state their request to avoid confusion? Sometimes, we unnecessarily complicate prayer. When the disciples asked Jesus how to pray, Christ provided them with a model prayer to use. It consists of straightforward language that lists everyday needs. Frequently, inmates ask me about prayer. They usually say something like, "How do I start? What exactly should I say?"

I tell them that prayers don't have to be pretty or poetic. Prayers should be personal rather than theological. The truth is that the Lord Jesus is never confused about what we need; it's up to us to be specific. How precise should we be in prayer? Well, as specific as we can. However, there are times when the pain is so deep and the need so great that words fall short of describing our request.

Nowhere in Scripture does it state that we need to pray eloquently or with carefully chosen words. It simply says we should pray, with only one requirement: we are to pray in the name of Jesus. Christ Himself confirmed this in John 14:13-14: *"And I will do whatever you ask in My name, so that the Father may be glorified in the Son. You may ask Me for anything in My name, and I will do it."* This is exactly what the ten lepers do when they cry out to Jesus in Luke 17:13, saying: *"Jesus, Master, have mercy on us."*

What I appreciate about this exchange between the lepers and Christ is that everyone else fades into the background. The disciples and the crowds remain silent. Any perceptions or prejudices against this group of diseased men are silenced. There are no interruptions or distractions. Similarly, in prayer, we experience uninterrupted communication with the Savior.

It doesn't matter where we are or how far we have strayed from God. He knows where we are and still hears us. God heard Jonah in the whale, Jeremiah in the pit, and Daniel in the lion's den. In the same way, we are always heard, especially when we cry out from the depths of our pain and suffering.

Have you ever found yourself in a situation where words like pity, help, and healing are difficult to express? Of course, you have. From time to time, we feel cut off, isolated, and forgotten—a faceless name in the crowd that no one seems to understand or care about. Sometimes we place ourselves there. Yet, our circumstances can confine us to this isolated place known as nowhere.

It's not a physical place, but more like an emotional wasteland. Feelings of disconnection, misunderstanding, and being ignored can happen to anyone. The Holy Spirit, sometimes referred to as the 'Hound of Heaven,' knows our scent and sniffs us out, wherever we go. The Lord found a frightened Adam and Eve hiding in the bushes and comforted them. God discovered Moses in that wilderness, giving him purpose. The Lord found a nervous Joshua on the eve of battle and granted him courage.

Jesus found the two heartbroken disciples on the Emmaus road, guiding them in the right direction. Christ freed Thomas from doubt, and Paul was liberated from his murderous intent on the Damascus Road. No matter where we are, even if we feel lost or afraid, Jesus finds us. This is effortless for Him because He never leaves us or gives up on us. Nothing on this earth, seen or unseen, can separate us from the love of God in Christ Jesus.

So then, Jesus will not forsake the ten men pleading for pity. Have you noticed that this healing miracle isn't immediate; it happens in stages? It is accomplished by the ten men who do what Jesus tells them to do. In verse 14, Jesus sees these men and tells them, **"Go, show yourselves to the priests."** Did you notice the comma after the word 'Go'? This means Christ's instructions are a two-step process. It isn't, *Go show yourselves to the priests.* Why would they do that since no healing has taken place? By saying, **"Go,"** He is asking them to get moving, even before the healing takes effect. Step out before the miracle becomes evident. Let your faith propel you forward before you have evidence that something is going to happen. Walk by faith; limp, if necessary, but start believing, which means start moving. More often than we would like, the Lord God calls us to live this way.

Jesus tells Thomas, **"Because you have seen me, you have believed; blessed are those who have not seen and yet have believed"** (John 20:29). The Lord does not call us to step out merely because we see Him doing something. God expects us to actively engage in our faith-walk because we believe the Lord can and will act. Not stepping out means sitting tight in our misery and clinging to hopelessness. Sometimes we can feel paralyzed by fear, but we should never be paralyzed in faith. True faith requires deliberate and intentional action that propels us forward.

Faith is never passive; it should always be an active force that shapes our lives and challenges us to believe in the goodness and grace of Almighty God, even before it happens. There should be a heartfelt conviction fueling our inner dialogue. Mark 11:24 says, **"Therefore I tell you, whatever you ask for in prayer, believe that you have received it, and it** *will be yours."* James 1:6 says, *"But when you ask, you must believe and not doubt."*

This means there are times when the Lord requires us to act on faith with immediate results, moving forward motivated by belief alone. This is what Jesus expects the lepers to do. Even before the miracle of healing begins, their faith must be active. If you're waiting for the Lord to prove Himself by giving you a guarantee that things will happen as you expect, you might be waiting a long time. You need to start believing and then get moving. You need to GO!

Fortunately, the ten people with leprosy who responded to the command to *"Go"* did just that. But let's not overlook the second part of Christ's command: *"show yourselves to the priests."* Show them what? Show off their leprosy? They weren't healed yet. This means that moving forward in belief requires expectation—not if God will do something, but when. Pray with your hands open, with the posture of expectation. Without expectation, belief isn't just dreaming.

*"Go"* and *"show"* are how Jesus tells them to proceed. What's remarkable is that's exactly what they do. There doesn't seem to be any hesitation on their part. Here we see faith in action—faith ignited by hope. Not the kind of faith that says, "Oh, well, I've got nothing to lose, let's give it a try." This kind of faith says if God is with me, who can be against me? If nothing can snatch me from my Father's hand, then nothing can hold me back except my reluctance to believe. On the other hand, if we hesitate, doubt can gain the upper hand, allowing fear to rule the day.

You will never experience a miracle by playing it safe. However, you will discover that wherever the Lord leads you is the absolute best place for you to be! Do you want proof? Here it is! ...**And as they went, they were cleansed** (Luke 17:14).

If these ten men hadn't stepped out, there would have been no healing miracle. They would have remained where they were, in that terrible place, enduring an endless cycle of misery and pain. If you want to break that cycle of misery in your life, then take God at His word by stepping out in faith. Stop waiting for the Lord to come to you; He is already here. Instead, ask the Lord what He wants you to do and where He wants you to go, and then move toward it. This is exactly what the ten lepers did, and as they went, they were healed. We should accept that the Lord God often works in stages and steps because spiritual growth is a process, not something immediate.

An ongoing, never-ending experience shaped by the circumstances and events of life. God uses everything to mold and transform us. Nothing is wasted. We are continually in the process of becoming—better people, better parents, better spouses, better Christians. The process initiated by God only concludes when this life on Earth is over. Until then, our role is to work in submission to the will of God so that we can be transformed by the renewing of our minds, which shapes and molds us into the image of Jesus Christ, our Lord and Savior.

God has a plan for each of us. A plan *with* a purpose. Call it a "goal," confirmed by Psalm 92:12-14, **The righteous will flourish like a palm tree, they will grow like a cedar of Lebanon; planted in the house of the Lord, they will flourish in the courts of our God. They will still bear fruit in old age, they will stay fresh and green.**

In Philippians 1:6 …***being confident of this, that He who began a good work in you will carry it on to completion until the day of Christ Jesus.***

Ephesians 2:10 NLT ***For we are God's masterpiece. He has created us anew in Christ Jesus, so we can do the good things He planned for us long ago.***

In our Christian walk, the Lord guides us in stages and steps. We need to embrace these stages and take these steps until the Lord brings us home as His finished masterpiece. Speaking of stages and steps, let's imagine how the miracle of the ten lepers' healing occurred. Did their diseased skin begin to tingle when the healing commenced? Did their balance return when their toes suddenly appeared? Were they watching their fingers grow? Or were they staring at one another when the healing set in? They witnessed open sores transform into smooth skin. If they didn't see it, they certainly felt it. Limbs were straightened and restored.

Now they feel the sun's warmth on new skin. The stench of decay disappears, replaced by the sweet scent of renewed health. Suddenly, limping turns into walking and then erupts into running. Crutches and canes fly into the air. Is that when the laughter began, and tears of joy started to flow? Certainly, that's when the memories of home began to rush in: thoughts of family and friends, a soft bed, and a hot meal. All of this lay ahead of them.

First stop: the temple for a priestly inspection, then straight home for a joyful reunion. The excitement of their joy propels them forward when, suddenly, one of the ten men slows down. The others call for him to hurry, but he comes to a complete stop. Realizing what has just happened to him, he stops looking at his healing. Then, he looks back. That's when he understands who is responsible. While the nine race back to their old lives, forgetting how this happened, this one man who remembers returns. He goes back to show gratitude in a deliberate, dramatic way. *He threw himself at Jesus' feet and thanked Him-and he was a Samaritan* (Luke 17:16).

Does God need our thanks? Not really. Does He want it? Absolutely. Just think, if every answered prayer we ever prayed was followed by a sincere thank you, we would often be overflowing with gratitude. But we aren't, are we? Like the nine rushing away, we are so busy with life that we barely find the time to say thank you to each other, let alone thank God. So, as this man returns with profound gratitude, listen to the disappointment in Jesus' words found in Luke 17:17-18, *Jesus asked, "Were not all ten cleansed? Where are the other nine? Has no one returned to give praise to God except this foreigner?"*

Can you hear the frustration in Jesus' voice? It seems a bit out of character for the Savior, doesn't it? Was Christ looking for a pat on the back or a round of applause? Certainly not; Jesus wants to give them more.

More than they had already received and even more than they had dreamed possible. The suffering in their bodies was significant, but the disease in their souls was even greater. It's the sting of sin that drives us apart and the scourge of sin driving us away from Almighty God. The gap widens when it collides with hate and hurt, fear and pain. All the things that drive us apart are the very same things Jesus comes to heal.

Jesus wants to do more than straighten out your life; He wants to heal your heart by redeeming your soul. Sadly, this is something the other nine never understood. They knew and believed in Jesus and were even touched by Him. However, they didn't give Christ the opportunity to do everything He came to do. They missed the greatest blessing available to them. Are you willing to let Jesus touch and heal every part of you, or just the parts you choose? If you want Jesus to heal all of you, then you must be willing to take your faith a step further. ***Then Jesus said to him, "Rise and go; your faith has made you well"*** (Luke 17:19).

The word "well" also means "whole." To be whole is to be saved, which goes beyond physical healing. God's plan is to save the world from sin.

John 3:17 confirms this, ***"For God did not send His Son into the world to condemn the world, but to save the world through Him."***

Real faith, saving faith, means believing that the world is lost and needs saving. God sent Jesus into the world to do that because we can't save ourselves. When you bring your sin to the Savior, sin is forgiven in and through Christ, as **"your faith makes you well"** (Luke 17:19). This means that faith is not just believing in something. Saving faith requires us to believe in someone, Jesus Christ, to experience the ultimate miracle that God has for us: the forgiveness of our sins and the saving of our souls.

Now you realize that this story is about more than a chance encounter between ten men in need of physical healing. It's about nine men who missed the opportunity of a lifetime and only one man who didn't. Nine men who settled for what they were given, while only one man received the ultimate miracle. In which group would you be found? Do you stand with the nine who never knew the saving grace of God, or do you kneel with the one man who was made whole, body and soul?

Every Sunday, there are people sitting in church who believe in Jesus and what He can do, but they've never understood that only Jesus saves them from their sins. They have yet to embrace the ultimate miracle of salvation by receiving Christ as their Savior. Does this describe you? If so, what are you ready and willing to do about it?

## Chapter 6 Questions

1. Why do we often miss the quiet pain and silent suffering that people endure?

2. Imagine and describe the experience of these men as they gave up their families. Write your thoughts.

3. How did these ten men find the courage to put their faith in Jesus' healing power?

4. Why is it important to pray in the name of Jesus? What does it signify?

5. Can we ever be so lost that God can't find us? So sinful that God can't forgive us? So hurt that God can't help us? If not, why not?

6. Sometimes God answers our prayers in steps and stages. Can you give an example from your life?

7. If you want things to change, what does faith require of you?

8. How can we cultivate a deeper sense of gratitude to God for all He does for us? List practical suggestions?

# Rich Young Ruler

## Mark 10:17-23

*As Jesus started on His way, a man ran up to Him and fell on his knees before Him. "Good Teacher," he asked, "what must I do to inherit eternal life?"*

*"Why do you call Me good?" Jesus answered. "No one is good—except God alone. You know the commandments: 'You shall not murder, you shall not commit adultery, you shall not steal, you shall not give false testimony, you shall not defraud, honor your father and mother.'"*

*"Teacher," he declared, "all these I have kept since I was a boy."*

*Jesus looked at him and loved him. "One thing you lack," He said. "Go, sell everything you have and give to the poor, and you will have treasure in Heaven. Then come, follow Me."*

*At this the man's face fell. He went away sad, because he had great wealth.*

*Jesus looked around and said to His disciples, "How hard it is for the rich to enter the kingdom of God!"*

Mark 10:17-23

THE MAN BEGINS ON THE RIGHT FOOT. He maintains the right posture and adopts the right approach. He possesses a clear understanding, fueled by well-defined motivation. On the surface, it's admirable and, to the untrained eye, commendable. He walks the walk and is quick to tell you, leaving nothing to the imagination about his spiritual condition.

*I'm good,* he believes, *better than most. Look at my life. My successes are undeniable. My achievements are highly commendable. I have more and have done more than most people dream of. Many people praise me; some dislike me, blinded by their jealousy. It doesn't matter because I'm out in front financially and spiritually. I have it all, and I've only just begun. Still, I must admit, something doesn't feel right; something is missing. There is one piece of the puzzle that escapes me.*

*Well, this Jesus of Nazareth has His head on straight. A smart guy with the gift of gab. People listen and seem to respect Him. Maybe He can help me find the missing piece to the puzzle or at least point me in the right direction. I'd better hurry up; it looks like He's getting ready to leave.*

**As Jesus started on His way, a man ran up to Him and fell on his knees before Him. "Good Teacher," he asked, "what must I do to inherit eternal life?"** (Mark 10:17)

Don't confuse this man's haste with humility. Dropping to one knee differs from a heart that is bowed in genuine self-reflection; his approach is completely self-serving.

Listen carefully to his question for Christ: ***"Good Teacher, what must I do to inherit eternal life?"*** In the same way there is no 'I' in the word team, there is no 'We' in salvation, redemption, or spiritual deliverance. Why not? There is nothing anyone can do to save themselves. Not a thing. Somehow, this man believes that he can get the job done. Sadly, he's looking for information, not truth. He believes he needs advice, not rescue. With the right set of facts coupled with careful execution, he can make it happen.

This man wasn't listening to what Christ just said about the little children back in Mark 14:14-15: ***"...Let the little children come to Me, and do not hinder them, for the kingdom of God belongs to such as these. Truly I tell you, anyone who will not receive the kingdom of God like a child will never enter it."***

What Jesus is saying comes down to just two words: 'helpless dependence.' A small child is helpless and dependent on someone to provide for and care for them. A 6-year-old child will never walk up to a parent and ask, "What can I do to help? You do the dishes, and I'll take out the trash. You make dinner while I mow the lawn."

It's ridiculous—so absurd, in fact, that Christ tries to jar the man's consciousness by saying, **"Why do you call Me good? No one is good except God alone"** (Mark 10:18).

The man believes he is good enough to save himself. He doesn't see himself as helpless but as capable—not dependent but independently able to redeem himself. *"What must I do to inherit eternal life?"* The emphasis is on himself.

Just point me in the right direction, and I'll figure things out by myself. Really? So, Jesus flips the script on this man by saying this, *"You know the commandments: 'You shall not murder, you shall not commit adultery, you shall not steal, you shall not give false testimony, you shall not defraud, honor your father and mother'"* (Mark 10:19).

*"Teacher,"* he declared, *"all these I have kept since I was a boy"* (Mark 10:20).

It's obvious that this man forgets the missteps he has taken along life's way. There was the time he pushed his sister to the ground, scraping her knee. There was the piece of fruit that found its way into his pocket when the merchant wasn't looking. There was the argument he had with his neighbor. There was the anger he felt when his teacher scolded him and when his father disciplined him. Have all his business dealings been clean and legitimate as an adult? Doubtful. All his lifelong indiscretions have been conveniently swept under the rug of his subconscious.

I know, let's not rush to judgment on this man; instead, let's give him the benefit of the doubt. He believes he is doing everything that's expected of him and has a high opinion of himself. You know people like him. They might be co-workers, neighbors, relatives, or even someone from church. Whenever they're around, they trumpet their achievements, boasting about their lives, personal accomplishments, or their kids. When you see them coming, you try to avoid them, hoping to keep the conversation short since it's always about them. They get on your nerves and under your skin.

Often, we walk away shaking our heads, wondering how someone could be so full of themselves. So, how does Jesus handle anyone who might be a legend in their own mind? Interestingly enough, Mark tells us in verse 21 exactly what Christ does: ***Jesus looked at him and loved him.*** Ouch! Aren't you glad that Jesus isn't like us? Christ never slams the door of annoyance or distances Himself from us. Jesus may not agree with the way we're living, but He's always accessible, always ready to give us the grace we need to get on track. Frequently, grace comes in the form of hearing the truth.

Sometimes, as a chaplain, I must dump a pail of cold water on someone by telling them the truth. The truth will set you free, but sometimes it will knock you down before you experience freedom. Recently, I was talking to an inmate named Carlos, who had a high opinion of himself. He proudly told me he was a Christian, describing himself as someone who lives out his faith by helping others and trying to be the kind of person God wants him to be. He also offered some excuses for being in jail. Ironically, I happened to be studying this passage, so I grabbed a Bible and read about the rich young ruler, focusing on what the man tells Jesus. When I finished, I looked at Carlos, who said, 'That guy sounds like me.' To which I replied, "If you were living the Christian life, what are you doing here?" Then, while looking down, he said, "Why am I sitting here wearing jail orange, talking to you?"

Carlos is a young man of 28, who has been convicted of rape and is awaiting sentencing. Next came the pail of cold water. "Carlos, you are where you are because you did what you did." When I told him that, he wept. As difficult as it was to hear, it's the only way for Carlos to find forgiveness from God and healing for his soul. No matter how many misconceptions or inflated opinions we have about ourselves, despite our exaggerated sense of self-worth that distorts the true picture of who we are, the Lord God, who loves us, never stops telling us the truth because the Lord never gives up on us. We shouldn't give up on the truth or on this world either. But I believe some Christians have thrown up their hands in disgust, believing that things are too far gone, while mouthing the words, "Come, Lord Jesus."

The reason our society suffocates beneath a culture of sin is that falsehood controls the narrative. When truth is pushed to the back of the line, deceit dominates. This happens because God's truth is ignored and suppressed, sometimes even by Christians. How? It's suppressed by our silence. The reason the world doesn't want to listen is because the Gospel message shatters the myth of self-sufficiency. The Gospel message drives a stake through the heart of self-righteousness. Here's how? *For it is by grace you have been saved, through faith— and this is not from yourselves; it is the gift of God— not by works, so that no one can boast* (Ephesians 2:8-9).

The Gospel says we can't, but God can. The Gospel says we won't, but God will. The Gospel says we're lost until we're found. Once found, we can still lose our way, because from time to time we tend to wander. We are all like sheep that have gone astray.

Someone might say, "I go to church regularly. I tithe and serve when and where I can. What more do you want?" The Lord doesn't want our spiritual aerobics. God wants our heart. The Lord expects to be first, which means His throne must be our heart. *"For where your treasure is, there your heart will be also"* (Matthew 6:21).

Our intentions must be for Him first. Our plans, hopes, and dreams must be guided and driven by Him for our plans to be blessed by Him. You can't live your life and let God in where He fits. The danger here is that anything can get in the way. Anything can push God out of the way. Whatever we lean on instead of God will cripple our desire to follow Him. The world is quick to prop us up with something other than God. Worldly success, financial security, beauty, brains—there is plenty to choose from. More than enough to throw anyone off track.

For the rich young ruler in the teaching, his possessions matter. The guy is loaded: a fancy home, luxury cars, and a wardrobe that rivals a Paris fashion show—Gucci, Armani, Dior galore. Have I mentioned his home? Let's open the large front door and behold a glistening marble floor. Overhead, a Tiffany chandelier twinkles with light, while fine art adorns the walls, and furniture comes from the finest stores. Not just a home, but a palace—spacious and luxurious, a dream home beyond your imagination. Ring the bell, and a servant will come to provide some costly libation. As humorous as this sounds, it wasn't funny for the rich young ruler when Christ answered his question, *"What must I do, to inherit eternal life?"* (Mark 10:17).

He thought it would be just another business transaction. But it isn't. He isn't ready for the truth. He never dreamed that his life would become a gigantic garage sale, with all the proceeds going to the poor. *"Go sell everything you have and give it to the poor, then you will have treasure in Heaven. Then come, follow Me"* (Mark 10:21). This is what Jesus meant when He said, *"One thing you lack."*

This is the moment when we can comfortably step back from this passage, believing it doesn't apply to us. No, this passage is for the rich and famous, the A-listers, the fat cats in government who get rich off their political connections. It's not for hard-working folks like us, trying to make ends meet. It's not for those on fixed incomes. The average person, feeling the weight of inflation, is overlooked when this chilling truth comes crashing down. Or is it?

If Jesus came to you and said, "One thing you lack." Would you respond, "Not me, Lord!" Or are you willing to accept the idea that you have something to give up? Are you ready to admit that something stands between you and Jesus?

This verse has a broader application than possessions. It applies to everything that blocks our view of Christ, preventing us from following hard after Him. It can be a practice, a belief, or an attitude that holds us back. Each of us has something in our lives that needs to be discarded.

The other day, I opened my fridge and smelled something that wasn't right. I looked around and moved things, but found nothing. The next day, when I opened the fridge, the smell was stronger. Still, I couldn't find the source of the pungent aroma. Later that day, my daughter was over, and I asked her to check the fridge. "Whoa, Dad!" she said. As she quickly pulled out a piece of uncooked chicken in a plastic container, hidden on the bottom shelf, that was the source of the odor. It quickly went into the trash.

Let me tell you a secret: Sin doesn't smell. Wrongdoing is odorless. Anger, unforgiveness, selfishness, and harsh judgment have no aroma. But that doesn't mean it can't stink to high heaven. Heaven is the place where the ungodly odor of our intentions is obvious. This is why we can't monitor our spiritual well-being, because the smell can escape us. We need help that can only come from the Lord, as spelled out in Psalm 139:23-24: ***Search me, God, and know my heart; test me and know my anxious thoughts. See if there is any offensive way in me and lead me in the way everlasting.***

The first thing regarding the commandments that this man fails to follow is the first commandment. It is written in Exodus 20:2-3, ***"I am the LORD your God, who brought you out of Egypt, out of the land of slavery. You shall have no other gods before Me."*** The reason the first commandment is placed first is that the rest of the commandments can't be obeyed unless we understand what the Lord has done and what the Lord expects from us. To be brought out of Egypt means to be free from the oppressive environment of this godless world. Salvation provides us with the ability to set our sights on things of eternal worth while understanding that the treasures of this world have no eternal value. As God's people, we are called out of the slavery of sin.

The Apostle Paul says this in Romans 6:17-18 (NLT), ***"Thank God! Once you were slaves of sin, but now you wholeheartedly obey this teaching we have given you. 18 Now you are free from your slavery to sin, and you have become slaves to righteous living."*** This means we are no longer helplessly trapped in sin. The truth is, when we sin, we choose to do so. "The devil made me do it" will not stand up in Heaven's court. Carlos' crime took place in a strip club. So, I asked him, "Do you think you can hang out in the devil's backyard and not have him hurt you?" As Christians, we have a target on our backs.

The devil loves nothing more than to get us in his sights so he can take us out. Satan can't steal our salvation, but he can wreck our lives if we let him. Carlos asked me if I thought any woman would ever want anything to do with him since he is now a felon who will be labeled a sex offender for the rest of his life. Forgiveness for sin is always possible, but the consequences of sinning may never go away. This is why hanging out in Egypt or at a strip club is begging for trouble.

Leaving Egypt means creating distance between ourselves and the spiritual traps of this world. It also involves moving on from a culture that dictates, demands, and undermines our sense of self-worth. No matter how much you have, money can't buy happiness. Eventually, possessions end up possessing us. Achievements, accolades, and applause will fade over time and diminish with age, leaving us empty-handed.

If you're a Minnesota Twins fan, you know the name Tony Oliva, who played from 1962 to 1976. During his career, Oliva received several awards, including Rookie of the Year and the Golden Glove Award. He won the batting title three times and had an impressive lifetime batting average of 304. He was inducted into the Baseball Hall of Fame on December 5, 2021. I saw Mr. Oliva at a Minnesota Vikings game. At 85 years old, he needs assistance to get around. Sadly, he is a mere shell of his former self; this can happen to anyone. It was poet and philosopher Henry David Thoreau who said, "Rather than love, than money, than fame, give me truth."

The truth will always bring into focus what is right, good, and what will endure for eternity. Even though the rich young ruler boasts about keeping all the commandments, he neglected the first commandment that concludes with, **"You shall have no other gods before Me"** (Exodus 20:3).

His wealth took God's place, neutralizing Heaven's grace. Recognizing this, Jesus serves up a serious portion of truth in Mark 10:21, *"One thing you lack."* It only takes one thing. Whatever we lack can hold us back spiritually. Whatever we rely on other than God will hinder our ability to follow Him. This is why Jesus tells the rich young ruler, "Get rid of your possessions, then come, follow me."

Always remember, Jesus isn't looking for leaders; He's looking for followers. Jesus isn't looking for dependable people; He's looking for individuals willing to depend on Him. Imagine the impact on a man who sees himself as wildly successful. He believes that he is within reach of securing eternal life. Once truth shines into his life, it becomes clear that he's light years away from his goal.

Christ's words hit him hard, revealed in Mark 10:22, *At this the man's face fell. He went away sad because he had great wealth.* He owned so much. So much owned him, leaving no room for God.

So, how do we determine if something is missing? How can we know for sure that we're living for Christ? Again, Jesus gives us the answer at the end of the passage in Mark 10:21, *"Follow Me."*

Are you diligently following Jesus, living as He lived and loving as He did? Are you consistently about your Heavenly Father's business, or have the demands of this world taken over your life? If you're uncertain, then ask the Lord what He thinks.

God cares deeply for you and will share the truth because His love for you is *so great* that He simply cannot withhold it.

## Chapter 7 Questions

1. The man in this story appears to have good intentions in his approach to Jesus. Are there any underlying problems evident from the start?

2. Is it fair for Jesus to expect Christians to have an attitude of "helpless dependence" in their spiritual lives?

3. Is honest self-appraisal an essential practice in the Christian faith? Please explain why or why not.

4. How can Jesus look at this man and love him, despite his inflated sense of self-importance? Are you able to do the same, or is there someone whose pride stands in the way? What should you do?

5. How does the Gospel message shatter the myth of self-sufficiency? What would happen if it did?

6. If someone said that Jesus was 'anti-rich,' how would you respond? What was Jesus trying to teach the wealthy young man?

7. Is it fair to say that with God, forgiveness is always possible, yet the consequence for sin is inescapable? Explain.

8. The Bible teaches that the truth will set you free, yet the rich young man doesn't seem free. Why is that?

# Chapter 8
# Blind Bartimaeus
## Mark 10:46-52

*Then they came to Jericho. As Jesus and His disciples, together with a large crowd, were leaving the city, a blind man, Bartimaeus (which means "son of Timaeus"), was sitting by the roadside begging. When he heard that it was Jesus of Nazareth, he began to shout, "Jesus, Son of David, have mercy on me!"*

*Many rebuked him and told him to be quiet, but he shouted all the more, "Son of David, have mercy on me!"*

*Jesus stopped and said, "Call him."*

*So they called to the blind man, "Cheer up! On your feet! He's calling you." Throwing his cloak aside, he jumped to his feet and came to Jesus.*

*"What do you want me to do for you?" Jesus asked him.*

*The blind man said, "Rabbi, I want to see."*

*"Go," said Jesus, "your faith has healed you." Immediately he received his sight and followed Jesus along the road.*

Mark 10:46-52

COME WITH ME INTO THE FIRST CENTURY. First of all, breakfast is not a priority. Once dressed, you head off to work, carrying a few figs and some bread to eat on the way. This eases your hunger until the evening meal, which consists of more bread, fish, and some fruit. So, while eating and walking through the streets of Jericho, blind Bartimaeus uses his free hand to feel his way by running it along the wall. He's also guided by the sounds of merchants opening their shops and the familiar bark of a dog during this routine trip from home. Eventually, he arrives at the city gate.

Counting his steps away from the city entrance, Bartimaeus quickly finds his usual spot—a flat patch of ground free of rocks. He always sits with his back to the sun. The branches of a nearby tree sway and scratch against each other on windy days. Bartimaeus sits cross-legged, draping his cloak over his lap. This cloak is Bartimaeus's most important possession, serving as protection against the weather or a blanket when he sleeps. It's also a valuable tool for his begging activities. Once Bartimaeus sits down, he makes a fist that pushes the cloak down into the hole of his lap, creating a pocket where people throw their coins. Now he's ready for business. Bartimaeus knows this is a profitable location due to the frequent travelers heading to and from Jerusalem, some fifteen miles away. Some people travel with children, who stop and stare at a blind man until their parents call them. Occasionally, a dog brushes against him, giving him a sniff.

Merchants pass by, leading their donkey-drawn carts, creaking and squeaking under the weight of their supplies. An occasional passerby tosses a coin or two into Bartimaeus' cloak-turned collection plate. The blind man can feel the coins hit his cloak; the sound and weight of these coins tell him their value. It might seem like a small thing, but I find it curious that Bartimaeus' blindness is mentioned before his name. It's not Bartimaeus the blind man; it's blind Bartimaeus.

We wouldn't say, 'There goes the Crippled Carl, or here comes Hearing-impaired Harry. So why emphasize Bartimaeus' blindness? This practice is not only insensitive; it is a formal accusation. Anyone in the first century who suffered from a disability or persistent medical condition was considered 'unclean.' Ongoing physical ailments were viewed as divine punishment for an ungodly life. In John 9:2, the disciples encounter a different man born blind. They ask Jesus, *"Rabbi, who sinned, this man or his parents, that he was born blind?"* The assumption is that this man's disability was a sure sign of God's judgment.

Furthermore, in Matthew 16, Jesus calls Simon Peter, Simon Bar-Jonah, which means Simon, son of a father named Jonah. This should not be confused with the Old Testament figure, Jonah. However, when we read the name Bartimaeus, the text tells us it means Son of Timaeus. Sadly, because Bartimaeus is such an insignificant character, we don't know his real name. Who's that blind guy over there? Oh, that's the Son of Timaeus.

Now, Bartimaeus isn't just blind; he's a beggar. He's viewed as a non-productive member of society, someone living off the hard work and benevolence of others. He gives nothing in return. All he does is take, take, take. His presence makes people feel uncomfortable, just like those individuals who stand on highway exit ramps, asking us for money.

They hold up signs that read "Homeless" or "Please Help, God bless you..." If the light is red, we don't make eye contact. But if we do look, we create backstories about them while waiting for the light to turn green. We assume that the guy wants money for alcohol or drugs. The young woman has a brand-new SUV parked a few blocks away. Likewise, people grow weary of seeing blind Bartimaeus in the same spot every day, begging for coins. Some individuals deliberately move to the other side of the road, as they see this beggar as a public nuisance.

On this day, Bartimaeus senses a large crowd leaving the city, so he asks what's going on. Someone tells him that Jesus of Nazareth is leaving the city, heading to Jerusalem. The mention of the Carpenter's name reminds Bartimaeus of the healing stories he's heard about this Jesus, prompting him to spring into action. **When he heard it was Jesus of Nazareth, he began to shout, "Jesus, Son of David, have mercy on me!"** (Mark 10:47). The term "Son of David" is a Messianic title, which indicates that Bartimaeus believes Jesus is the Christ, the Anointed One sent as the Redeemer of the world. How Bartimaeus arrives at this conclusion is amazing. It's ironic that blind Bartimaeus can see the identity of Christ long before some of Jesus' disciples can. However, what happens next is both sad and disturbing: I'm referring to the crowd's reaction to this blind beggar's attempt to connect with Jesus. In verse 48, it states, **Many rebuked him and told him to be quiet.**

Why did the crowd react this way? Because this was Blind Bartimaeus, who was considered a useless member of society, with no redeeming value or worth. His blindness was his badge of social and spiritual dishonor; it labeled him. Sadly, the labels we place on people blind us to who they truly are, preventing us from seeing their real value or worth. Furthermore, labels not only blind us, but they also divide us. Unfortunately, we have become a society obsessed with labels, filled with factions that are turned in on themselves. Often, we're pressured to take a stand because these opposing groups strike an emotional chord within us.

Here are a few conflicting positions: some are old, while others are new. Progressive or conservative? Defund the police or support the police? Pro-choice or pro-life? Open borders or closed borders? Pro-gay rights or no gay rights? More gun control or less gun control? Critical Race Theory or no Critical Race Theory? Every day, the list grows longer while the anger intensifies.

When we look at people through a political lens, through the lens of social issues, or through any lens at all, it prompts us to label them. This gives us a distorted perspective because all we see are labels, forgetting the person behind them. Now, I wish I could say this doesn't happen in church, but we all know it does. Unity of Spirit and harmony of intent are essential for the Body of Christ. This not only defines who we are, but it also sets us apart from the world. Jesus said this in John 13:35, ***"By this everyone will know you are My disciples, if you love one another."*** I'm convinced that Christianity isn't about being right; it's about showing love. If you want someone to take you seriously and listen to what you have to say, they must believe you care about them. If we don't care for the people sitting next to us, we'll never care for the people outside the walls of some church.

The way we treat each other serves as our spiritual credentials, giving us the ability to show the world that the Church is a different place, a place of acceptance, understanding, and grace. No one has life all figured out. You can't follow Jesus unless you know Him; even then, it's not easy. When we engage in labeling, we are no different from the world, no different from the crowd that told Bartimaeus to be quiet. Like them, we become a barrier instead of a bridge between Jesus and someone who needs Him—an ugly, angry voice rejecting people by slapping labels on them. God's people must abstain from labeling anyone at any time, because those labels discredit our witness and destroy the Gospel message. If there's anything I've learned as a chaplain over the last six years, it's that no one's life is neat, tidy, and squeaky clean. No one.

Recently, I talked to an inmate named Jason, who is facing a sentence of "no more than 40 yrs." Imagine being in your thirties and knowing you might not get out of jail until you're a senior citizen. Let me tell you about Jason. He grew up in a Christian home with a loving mother and father who had strong family values. This family attended church regularly, where Jason's father was an Elder.

As a child, Jason remembers his parents having Bible studies in their home. Jason attended Sunday School and Youth Group. At the age of twelve, he participated in a youth retreat at a Christian camp. This was when Jason gave his life to Christ. Yes, Jason is a Christian. Shocking, isn't it? Should we label Jason a murderer? Labels might describe someone, but they shouldn't define who they are unless we choose to see only the label and not the person behind it. Sometimes, you must fight back by resisting the labels people put on you. That's exactly what Bartimaeus does by refusing to remain quiet. He pushes back against the crowd's attempt to silence him. Shouting louder, he says, "**Son of David, have mercy on me!**" (Mark 10:48). Whatever you do, don't rush past the first two words of verse 49. It says, **Jesus stopped...**

Here is the Son of God, headed for Jerusalem, zeroing in on the culmination of His earthly ministry. And yet, **Jesus stopped...** Soon, Christ will endure an unjust trial and a gruesome beating, followed by His death, burial, and resurrection. We're talking about the redemption of the world, and still, **Jesus stopped.** Like storm clouds on the horizon, the forces of evil gather at Calvary, but they will have to wait. The nails that pierce Him, along with the mallet that will pound them through His flesh, must lie dormant at the bottom of some wooden box. The whip, the crown of thorns, the purple cape, and the cross will linger because some no-name, nobody, on the edge of that crowd cried out, so **Jesus stopped.**

Why did Christ stop? Jesus stopped because we have a God who cares for the poor and brokenhearted. Jesus stopped because we have a Savior who hears and responds to our every cry. The proof of these promises is confirmed by what the Savior does next. It says **Jesus stopped and said, "Call him."**

Today, if Jesus called you, would you hear Him? Or would your present circumstances drown out the Savior's voice?

Have you bought into the lie that you will never be good enough, so you don't deserve God's blessing? Don't let the voices of rejection get between you and the Savior. Rise up and push past those obstacles to receive what the Lord God wants to give you. I find it shamefully ironic that those who were trying to silence Bartimaeus suddenly changed their tune. In Mark 10:49, it reads, *So, they called to the blind man, "Cheer up! On your feet! He's calling you."*

Sometimes the same people who slap you down one minute can turn around and pat you on the back the next. Let's not focus on what those people are doing. Instead, take note of Bartimaeus and his determination to get to Jesus. How do we know that Bartimaeus is resolute and will not be denied? Look at verse 50, *Throwing his cloak aside, he jumped to his feet and came to Jesus.*

First off, people who are sight-impaired don't haphazardly throw things aside. If they did, they would have a tough time finding them again. This cloak is an important part of Bartimaeus's begging strategy, and it could have contained money. If it did, Bartimaeus doesn't care about the cloak or the coins he's throwing away. Why not? It's because Bartimaeus knows that Jesus has something better for him, better than what the world can offer. He doesn't want anything to come between him and the Savior. Is there anything standing between you and Jesus this morning? Anything holding you back from receiving *immeasurably more than all we* [you] *ask or imagine?* (Ephesians 3:20). If there is something getting in the way, you must let it go. You can't follow Jesus unless you are willing to toss aside anything that's holding you back. Clearly, Bartimaeus is willing to do that. Are you?

In verse 49, Christ tells the crowd to call Bartimaeus. At the end of Mark 10:50, it says Bartimaeus *came to Jesus.* This means the crowd is standing between Christ and the blind man. Thus, the crowd must part, and someone has to take

Bartimaeus by the arm, leading him to Christ. Would you have been that person?

All of us would like to think so. There is one way to know for sure. When was the last time you told someone about Jesus? The last time you shared with someone how you met Jesus and how that meeting changed your life. You don't have to be a theologian or a Billy Graham-like evangelist. You just need to give your testimony by sharing your story. Your story is unique. No one else in the world has your story. No one can tell your story but you. What people do with the story you tell them is between them and God. Once you share it with them, you have fulfilled your responsibility as a witness. This means that the last time you introduced someone to Jesus was the last time you shared your story. How long has it been? No one outside your church knows you're a Christian just because you show up on Sunday.

It's important to share your story out there, where those who truly need to hear it are waiting. They're your neighbors, co-workers, friends, and even family members. Once you trust in the power of your story and begin to share it, step back, and you'll be amazed at what happens next. When people encounter Jesus, miraculous things happen. Lives are changed. Didn't meeting Jesus change your life? After you make the introduction between Jesus and the Bartimaeus in your life, it's between them and the Savior. This introduction occurs when you share your story. Notice how Christ gets straight to the point with Bartimaeus (Mark 10:51), ***"What do you want me to do for you?" Jesus asks.*** Bartimaeus is equally direct, saying, ***"Rabbi, I want to see."*** We should note that Bartimaeus approaches Christ with a believing expectation. One way to determine if you have believing expectations is to examine your prayer life. Do you pray only when things

112

get completely out of hand? Do you ever say, "Well, there's nothing we can do, so we might as well pray"? Prayer should be our first response, not our last resort. Believing expectation means trusting that God can and will meet your needs, regardless of the circumstance.

Praying is our dialogue of dependence on the Lord, fueled by persistent trust. This is exactly what the Savior expects from us, confirmed by His response to Bartimaeus. *"Go," said Jesus, "your faith has healed you." Immediately, he received his sight and followed Jesus along the road* (Mark 10:52).

Even though Bartimaeus persevered against a prejudicial crowd, he still needed someone to guide him to Christ. People will never become followers of Jesus unless someone leads them to the Savior. However, certain things can get in the way, like labels. Never forget that labels blind us to the worth and value in others. Labels always diminish the Gospel message. We must be a bridge to Jesus, not a barrier. We need to see people as the Lord does. Either they are lost or saved. Those are the only descriptions that matter because they are eternal.

Don't underestimate the power of your salvation story. What you experienced changed you forever. Your story can introduce others to Jesus, allowing them to experience the same spiritual transformation that leads to salvation. Remember, this world has no hope without the Truth. The Truth isn't just an idea or a concept; it is the person of Jesus Christ. *"I am the Way, the Truth and the Life," Jesus said; "no one comes to the Father except through Me"* (John 14:6).

However, before anyone can come *to* Jesus, they must first be brought *to* Him. This happens when we tell someone who Jesus Christ is and what He has done for us. This world is a lost and hurting place, and everyone in it needs a Savior. *But how can they call on Him to save them unless they believe in Him? And how can they believe in Him if they have never heard about Him? And how can they hear about Him unless someone tells them?* (Romans 10:14 NLT).

SO, GO TELL THEM.

## Chapter 8 Questions

1. Do you think that the way we view others impacts our outreach efforts? If so, how?

2. It's easy to overlook those in need based on their approach. How can we prevent this?

3. Do we live in a society where it is evident that people are labeled? Does the Church label individuals?

4. How can we overcome our tendency to rush to judgment about others?

5. Have you ever tried to shake off the label that someone slapped on you? Did it work? What was your thought process?

6. Is there anything in your life that is drowning out the Savior's voice? What habit, practice, or belief are you reluctant to throw aside that's preventing you from experiencing the fullness of Jesus?

7. Are there any differences between evangelizing and witnessing? If so, please explain.

# A Garden Encounter

John 18:1-11

Luke 22:51

When He had finished praying, Jesus left with His disciples and crossed the Kidron Valley. On the other side there was a garden, and He and His disciples went into it.

Now Judas, who betrayed Him, knew the place, because Jesus had often met there with His disciples. So Judas came to the garden, guiding a detachment of soldiers and some officials from the chief priests and the Pharisees. They were carrying torches, lanterns, and weapons.

Jesus, knowing all that was going to happen to Him, went out and asked them, "Who is it you want?"

"Jesus of Nazareth," they replied.

"I am He," Jesus said. (And Judas the traitor was standing there with them.)

When Jesus said, "I am He," they drew back and fell to the ground. Again He asked them, "Who is it you want?"

"Jesus of Nazareth," they said.

*Jesus answered, "I told you that I am He. If you are looking for Me, then let these men go"*

*This happened so that the words He had spoken would be fulfilled: "I have not lost one of those you gave Me."*

*Then Simon Peter, who had a sword, drew it and struck the high priest's servant, cutting off his right ear. (The servant's name was Malchus.)*

*Jesus commanded Peter, "Put your sword away! Shall I not drink the cup the Father has given me?"*

John 18:1-11

*But Jesus answered, "No more of this!" And he touched the man's ear and healed him.*

Luke 22:51

DO YOU REALIZE THAT THERE WAS A MOMENT IN TIME when Easter was almost canceled? A sudden act by a single man nearly jeopardized the event of Resurrection Day. To explain, I need to tell you a story about two gardens. The first garden is a perfect place, filled with perfect people, or so it seems. This garden is called Eden. The second garden has its share of difficulties because of some problematic individuals. This is the Garden of Gethsemane. One day in that first garden, the enemy finds an opening in the hedge, allowing evil to slither through: belly down, with a darting tongue and cold, hungry eyes. In the second garden, evil boldly walks in upright, in the body of a man, leading other men in a sinister plot of betrayal.

In this first garden, evil has no name, only the shape of a snake. In the second garden, evil carries many names: Satan, Lucifer, Father of Lies, Judas. In the first garden, Adam and Eve take a terrible fall. In the second garden, the Son of Man takes a courageous stand.

In Eden, Satan uses a particular fruit tree to deceive Adam and Eve. At another location outside Gethsemane, Jesus is nailed to a different tree that delivers humanity. While Satan appears to succeed in the first garden, he ultimately fails in the second. How did he fail? The Evil One's attempt to bring suffering and death produces healing and life. Instead of drenching the world in shame in Gethsemane, the Devil sets the stage for a downpour of heavenly grace. In Eden, Satan seeks to destroy the bond between God and humanity. In Gethsemane, Jesus endeavors to restore the connection between Heaven and mankind. Eden may have represented Satan's momentary victory; however, Gethsemane is where the eternal victory is initiated. This conflict begins when Jesus and His disciples leave the upper room. John 18:1, **When He finished praying, Jesus left with His disciples and crossed the Kidron Valley. On the other side, there was an olive grove, and He and His disciples went into it.**

Heading out through the East Gate of Jerusalem, Jesus leads His disciples down a familiar path to a garden that stretches across a hillside known as the Kidron Valley. Frequently, Jesus uses this garden as a place of retreat. Here, you will find rows of olive trees standing guard like silent sentries. Olive trees are typically short, with thick barrel-like trunks and knurled, tangled branches. At night, these trees pot-mark the ground with large shadows that play tricks on your eyes. However, there might be more to those shadowy silhouettes than just the absence of light. Could it be that things from another world lurk in the recesses of those shadows?

Ungodly things are waiting, watching, and hoping that hell will gain the advantage in this second garden, as it did in the first. Now, with the battle lines drawn, it won't be long before this garden sanctuary becomes the stage where the cosmic battle between good and evil unfolds.

On this evening, Jesus and His followers find their familiar spot among the trees. Oddly, John doesn't mention the disciples sleeping or refer to Christ's prayers of emotional distress. Instead, he delivers a fast-forward narrative that takes us back to the city, where a group of Roman soldiers joins forces with a handful of temple guards. Leading this heavily armed posse is a Satan-indwelled Judas Iscariot. They follow him out of the city and down the winding road to Gethsemane. Judas knows the exact spot where Christ goes. The problem is it's nighttime, when Gethsemane's shadows can make identification difficult. Therefore, Judas leads the way, planning to identify Jesus with a predetermined signal: a kiss, or more precisely, the flickering caress of a snake.

Here we go again, another garden, the same snake, but this time with a different outcome. Verse 3, *So Judas came to the grove, guiding a detachment of soldiers and some officials from the chief priests and Pharisees*. Some translations use the word 'detachment' or 'cohort,' which includes 600 soldiers.

The Latin word used here is "maniple," which seems more reasonable since it refers to 60-120 armed men. To be cautious, we'll say 90 armed Roman soldiers. There are also temple guards present, representing the temple leader's authority. Their number is unknown, so let's estimate it at 5. Now let's add a few curious onlookers. We can confidently estimate that when Judas marches out of Jerusalem heading toward Gethsemane, he leads a force of at least 100 men.

This formidable group is heavily armed, as Roman soldiers usually carry swords, daggers, and, depending on the situation, a lance or a spear. They also wear body armor and hold shields. These men are highly trained, battle-hardened fighters with no regard for human life. Down from the city they come, torches blazing, armor rattling, lanterns swinging, armed to the teeth, marching in single file in the dead of night. Following the road's curves, they slink back and forth in true reptile-like fashion, with the Serpent from hell leading the way.

Now, imagine what the disciples see when Jesus wakes them up. The garden is ablaze with torchlight held by armed troops on full battle alert. Judas, aka the devil, is leading this small army that slowly encircles the drowsy disciples and the waiting Savior.

There also seems to be an ominous presence in the air. Amplified by the noise of creaking branches and swaying limbs, putting everyone's nerves on edge.

It's the same sensation when your doorbell rings in the middle of the night. You're awakened by that unmistakable sound, but did you hear it or dream it? So, you lie there quietly. Then the bell rings again. Who would come to your house at this late hour? You put on a robe and quietly head to the front door when suddenly someone starts pounding on the door. The banging scares you, causing your heart to race and your mouth to go dry. You can't see outside because you forgot to replace that burned-out bulb on the front porch. Finally, you summon the courage to ask, "Who is it?"

Gethsemane is no different, except the approaching mob didn't surprise the Savior. John makes this clear in verse 4: ***Jesus, knowing all that was going to happen to Him, went out and asked, "Who is it you want?"*** Let's read the first part of verse 4 again: ***<u>Jesus, knowing all that was going to happen to Him.</u>***

The Savior knew exactly how things would play out, and this same Divine awareness is active today. Jesus knows everything that is going to happen to us. There are no surprises for the Creator of the Universe, who controls every event—past, present, and future. Nothing will happen that can ever catch the King of Kings off guard. Satan's wildest schemes can't outsmart the Lord of Heaven and Earth. However, if Jesus knew what was going to happen to Him, then why did He ask them, **"Who do you want?"** Let's compare and contrast the two gardens once again. Let's focus on the male leads in each garden, as the Apostle Paul does in 1 Corinthians 15:45, 47 with these words: **So, it is written: The first man, Adam, became a living being; the last Adam a life-giving spirit.** Verse 47: **The first man was of the dust of the earth, the second Man from Heaven.**

In Gethsemane, the contrast between the first and last Adam continues to set them apart. The First Adam does nothing to protect his wife, Eve, from evil. However, the Last Adam steps up and confronts evil to protect those He loves. Where the First Adam fails, the Last Adam succeeds in fulfilling His promises of protection found in John 10:28 **"I give them eternal life, and they shall never perish; no one will snatch them out of My hand."**

Tragically, the first Adam's silence leads to his downfall, whereas the Last Adam's verbal directness causes the arresting mob to take a step back. When Jesus asks, (John 18:4) **"Who do you want?"** the mob replies in verse 5, **"Jesus of Nazareth." "I am He,"** Jesus said. **(And Judas the traitor was standing there with them.)**

John goes out of his way to mention Judas, emphasizing that Judas is the betrayer who is inhabited by Satan, as recorded at the Last Supper in John 13:27. **As soon as Judas took the bread, Satan entered him.**

So, let's review the composition of the mob that comes to arrest Christ. There is a Satan-possessed Judas. The temple guards are there, eager to fulfill the Pharisees' wishes to capture Jesus. Also present are approximately 90 heavily armed Roman soldiers, willing to do whatever it takes to make this happen. Additionally, there are a few nosy onlookers who came along for the ride, one named Malchus. It's quite a crowd that marches into that garden that night.

What happens in John 18:6 is nothing short of miraculous, mingled with the comical. **When Jesus said, "I am He,"** John tells us **...they drew back and fell to the ground.** Do you understand what just happened? The mere sound of Christ's voice acts like a flick on a lead domino, knocking back the crowd that crashes to the ground in this comical scene of chaotic confusion.

Imagine, as the lead person, Judas becomes so startled by Christ's directness that he rocks back on his heels, tumbling backward into 100 men, who collapse into a heap of bodies, lanterns, weapons, and torches. Together, the temple police and the daunting legionaries crumble into an undignified pile of manpower. Even Satan, the celebrated dark prince, is flat on his back. How embarrassing! Why did this formidable force wind up in a clumsy, humiliating pile of military might? It happens because of what Christ said back in John 10:18 (NLV): Jesus said, **"No one can take My life from Me. I sacrifice it voluntarily. For I have the authority to lay it down when I want to and also to take it up again. For this is what My Father has commanded."**

Christ's statement affirms God's authority to orchestrate the events of this world. Jesus cannot be taken by force; He willingly surrenders when He's good and ready. This is all part of His Father's redemption plan for humanity. This is your Jesus speaking—the all-powerful Son of God who sweeps aside anything that opposes Heaven's will. Nothing can stand against Him: not sickness or death, not financial or relational problems, not governments or military force. Nothing in all creation can resist the supernatural power of Jesus Christ! When the Great "I AM" opens His mouth, everything trembles and crashes to the ground! The Dark Prince is no match for the blinding presence of the Light of the World. This time, when Satan walks into the second garden, he doesn't have a leg to stand on, ending up flat on his back, just like the true snake that he is.

This proves that Satan is powerless to harm those whom the Savior protects. This is confirmed in John 18:7-9 as the conversation continues between Jesus and those trying to arrest Him. ***Again, He said to them, "Who is that you want?" And they said, "Jesus of Nazareth." "I told you that I am He," Jesus answered. "If you are looking for Me, then let these men go."***

Here, Jesus stands toe to toe with evil, shutting down Satan and the crack troops of the Roman guard while giving orders. Jesus' presence ensures the safety of His followers, as He predicted back in John 6:39 when He said, ***"And this is the will of Him who sent Me. I shall lose none of all that He has given Me, but raise them up on the last day."***

When Jesus says He will keep us safe, He keeps His word. Even if Hell wants us, it will have to go through Him to get to us. Satan tried that once in the first garden, with short-lived success. In the second garden, everything changes as the forces of evil are no match for the power of God's only Son. Hell can't manage what Christ can dish out. Jesus didn't save us so that we could become helpless targets of evil. In every circumstance, Christ has the Enemy under his thumb and the situation under control. Jesus is our fortress, our strong tower to which we run for shelter and protection.

Unfortunately, as Jesus' followers stand behind Him, one man decides to take control. Shockingly, Simon Peter leaps over the fence of common sense and does the unthinkable. Listen carefully to John 18:10-11: ***Then Simon Peter, who had a sword, drew it and struck the high priest's servant, cutting off his right ear.***

Let's try to envision what Simon Peter sees that night. Suddenly, the garden is ablaze with light, as torches and swinging lanterns cast shadows in all directions. The night air is filled with the sound of Roman boots marching through the wet grass while armed soldiers surround them. Peter notices some of the temple guards who caused them trouble whenever Jesus was in the temple are also in the crowd. Then he sees Judas Iscariot grinning with a devilish smile of wicked delight, leading this arresting mob toward the Savior. Peter panics, fearing for the safety of Jesus and the disciples.

This shocking reality fuels Simon's rage, compelling him to take action. He draws his weapon while yelling and swinging wildly at the person closest to him, causing Peter to cut off the ear of the high priest's servant. Imagine if he had wounded a Roman soldier? It could have triggered a massacre by a group of highly trained killers who would have killed Simon Peter and who knows who else.

Satan would have won a more decisive battle in the second garden than in the first. So, why did this happen? It occurred because one man, acting on his own free will, believes he knows more than God does. One man thinks he can do more than God can.

Why would Simon Peter believe he could single-handedly defeat this heavily armed force and the devil himself, all alone? Clearly, Peter is the poster child for impulsive behavior. Can you relate to him? I can. More often than not, we take our cues from Peter, don't we? We get ahead of the Lord Jesus, trying to fight life's battles on our own, attempting to control the uncontrollable.

Remember:

**The LORD is the one who goes ahead of you; He will be with you. He will not fail you or forsake you. Do not fear or be dismayed.** Deuteronomy 31:8 NASB1995

**The LORD your God who goes before you will Himself fight on your behalf...** Deuteronomy 1:30 NASB1995

**For the LORD will go before you, the God of Israel will be your rear guard.** Isaiah 52:12

**"I will go before you and will level the mountains; I will break down gates of bronze and cut through bars of iron."** Isaiah 45:2

This means that your life isn't a series of random occurrences, but a Divinely constructed plan. Therefore, we need to accept God's plan. It's not about being on the same page with God; it's about stepping back and letting the Lord turn the pages. Don't make the mistake of getting out in front of Christ, since that's where Satan will be happy to meet you and beat you by luring you into a fight you can't win.

By the way, Malchus never saw it coming. He never expected Peter to lunge at him from the shadows while making a sweeping gesture with his arm. In a flash, Malchus feels pain on the side of his head. Instinctively, his hand cups the place where his ear once was. Now, Malchus feels the flow of warm blood seeping through his fingers.

Fortunately, for Simon Peter's sake, Christ intervenes before it's too late. ***Jesus commanded Peter, "Put your sword away! Shall I not drink the cup the Father has given me?"*** (John 18:11).

Can you see Jesus grabbing Peter and pulling him back just before the Romans launch a counterattack? Who else might have been wounded or even killed? Everyone present is frozen in shock, unable to move. This is when Jesus steps forward, bending down to pick up the man's ear. Then Jesus cups the side of the high priest's servant's head, miraculously reattaching the man's severed ear, as if gently putting a fallen petal back on a flower.

Only after Jesus heals the servant's ear does the threat of retaliation stop. I wonder how this impacted Malchus. How could he not be deeply touched by Christ's healing touch? Did the blood ever wash out of his tunic? Did his hearing improve? Could he ever forget what happened that night in the garden? What do you think?

There was so much more happening here than anyone realizes. This was when a garden encounter in Eden connected with Christ's commanding presence and healing power, culminating in Gethsemane that night; this is just the beginning.

Never forget that ***Jesus, knowing all that was going to happen to Him,*** (John 18:4), indicates that the events leading up to His arrest, trial, and execution are no surprise. Even Simon Peter's impulsive act is expected. All of this is part of God's plan to restore us to grace and reclaim us as His own. The battle turned for Heaven that night in the garden.

On the cross, the battle was won. Unlike Peter, we must step back instead of trying to control our lives because the Lord God *is in control*. Jesus can manage whatever happens today, tomorrow, and forever. His plan for you is one you can rely on because Jesus is a Savior you can trust.

We're told in Proverbs 3:5, **Trust in the Lord with all your heart and do not lean on your own understanding;** because understanding doesn't provide peace. There is always something else coming along that will disrupt that peace. Sometimes, life can feel like an endless parade of problems, leaving us exhausted. For this reason, belief must take root in trust. There is a difference between belief and trust. Belief is a state of mind, whereas trust means aligning our actions with God's intentions.

This happens only when we continuously ask the Lord what we should do next. Always remember that the Lord isn't looking for leaders; Jesus wants followers, people willing to follow His plan. Christ isn't looking for dependable people; the Savior wants individuals willing to depend upon Him. So, don't rush ahead of the Lord. Instead, stay behind Jesus because this is the safest place you can be.

## Chapter 9 Questions

1. Why did Adam and Eve fall prey to the devil's deceit?

2. What did Adam and Eve hope to gain by eating the forbidden fruit?

3. What did the serpent hope to accomplish in the Garden of Eden?

4. When Judas brought the arresting party into Gethsemane, how many people accompanied him? Why did he need so many?

5. If we believe that Christ is in control of all things, how should we live each day? How are you doing?

6. What could have been the outcome of Peter assaulting Malchus, the high priest's servant?

7. Like Adam and Eve, Peter attempted to control the uncontrollable. Is this something you often find yourself doing?

8. When Christ healed Malchus, did He reattach the severed ear or create a new one? Why is this important?

# Chapter 10
# Looking for the Wrong Jesus

John 20:1-18

*Early on the first day of the week, while it was still dark, Mary Magdalene went to the tomb and saw that the stone had been removed from the entrance. So she came running to Simon Peter and the other disciple, the one Jesus loved, and said, "They have taken the Lord out of the tomb, and we don't know where they have put him!"*

*So Peter and the other disciple started for the tomb. Both were running, but the other disciple outran Peter and reached the tomb first. He bent over and looked in at the strips of linen lying there but did not go in. Then Simon Peter came along behind him and went straight into the tomb. He saw the strips of linen lying there, as well as the cloth that had been wrapped around Jesus' head. The cloth was still lying in its place, separate from the linen. Finally, the other disciple, who had reached the tomb first, also went inside. He saw and believed. (They still did not understand from Scripture that Jesus had to rise from the dead.) Then the disciples went back to where they were staying.*

*Now Mary stood outside the tomb crying. As she wept, she bent over to look into the tomb and saw two angels in white, seated where Jesus' body had been, one at the head and the other at the foot. They asked her, "Woman, why are you crying?" "They have taken my Lord away," she said, "and I don't know where they have put Him."*

*At this, she turned around and saw Jesus standing there, but she did not realize that it was Jesus. He asked her, "Woman, why are you crying? Who is it you are looking for?"*

*Thinking He was the gardener, she said, "Sir, if you have carried Him away, tell me where you have put Him, and I will get Him."*

*Jesus said to her, "Mary."*

*She turned toward Him and cried out in Aramaic, "Rabboni!" (which means "Teacher").*

*Jesus said, "Do not hold on to Me, for I have not yet ascended to the Father. Go instead to My brothers and tell them, 'I am ascending to My Father and your Father, to my God and your God.'"*

*Mary Magdalene went to the disciples with the news: "I have seen the Lord!" And she told them that He had said these things to her."*

John 20-1-18

THERE IS A QUIET, EERIE STILLNESS IN THAT PLACE. The sunrise has driven away the morning shadows. After the earthquake, the angel rolls away the stone. Once the Roman sentries regain consciousness and flee, it's quiet and still as the Son of God walks victoriously out of the tomb. You would expect some fanfare, a chorus of trumpets announcing the Resurrection.

But there is nothing. Shortly after, a solitary figure —a woman walking slowly —enters the cemetery.

This is the second time Mary Magdalene has shown up. She was there earlier, the first one to discover the stone rolled away. It sent shockwaves of panic through her, prompting Mary to run back to tell the disciples (verse 2), *"They have taken the Lord out of the tomb, and we don't know where they have put Him!"*

Now Mary returns, sobbing uncontrollably. As she stands outside, she looks in and sees two angels dressed in white sitting there. It never occurs to Mary to ask who they are or why they're there. You can't blame her since she's blinded by grief and the shock of loss. So the angels ask her, *"Woman, why are you crying?"* Mary tells them the same thing she tells the disciples.

*"They have taken away my Lord away," she said, "and I don't where they put Him"* (verse 13).

The reason Mary believes the remains of Jesus are stolen is that she is searching for the *wrong* Jesus. She's looking for a corpse, not the Resurrected Christ. Furthermore, Mary said twice that *"They have taken away my Lord..."* Who is Mary referring to? Is she talking about the Roman authorities, or does she think the Jewish religious leaders are responsible? Could Mary be referring to the Prince of Darkness and his demonic army? Does she believe that evil is behind this grave robbery?

Tragically, Mary has firsthand exposure to the destructive intentions of evil. In Luke 8:1-2, we read this, *After this, Jesus traveled from one town and village to another, proclaiming the good news of the kingdom of God. The Twelve were with Him, and also some women who had been cured of evil spirits and diseases: Mary (called Magdalene) from whom seven demons had come out.*

If Mary believes the 'powers of darkness' are responsible, then it seems that evil has triumphed once more, just as it did in her past life when she was tormented by her demon oppressors. Only Jesus could save her from those haunting voices inside her head, prompting her to do horrible, unspeakable things. Only Jesus could deliver her from those seven demonic jailers, who imprisoned her body and soul in that hellish torment. Jesus did just that, making Mary eternally grateful and forever committed to serving her Savior.

Now, as Mary is consumed by grief-stricken loss, she feels compelled to rescue Christ's remains from whoever or whatever has taken Him. Now we begin to understand why

Mary is looking for the wrong Jesus. We can only guess how she feels as she walks through that cemetery, searching for Christ's remains. This is the same Jesus who has been Mary's deliverer and protector, but is now dead and gone, leaving Mary vulnerable without her Shield and Defender. She may have thought that evil would come back for her, taking control like before, while inflicting the same hellish torment she once endured—abusing her, using her, ultimately wanting to kill her. At that moment, Mary must have felt like a child trapped in a tornado-like storm, a victim caught in the catastrophic consequences of Christ's death.

Let's talk about the events surrounding Christ's death. It is written, **Some of the women were watching from a distance. Among them was Mary Magdalene...** (Mark 15:40). Mary was an eyewitness to this terrible scene from start to finish. She sees all the gruesome details: the nail-pierced wounds and Christ's swollen face, blood-red from the beating and crown of thorns. She watches His chest heaving in painful spasms. Then, when Jesus breathed his last, Mary must have gasped as she descended into the darkness of her grief because the Light of the World had gone out.

So, for the second time this morning, Mary came to the cemetery in tears. But no one cares about her sorrow. Peter and John, consumed by their own emotional distress, seem to disregard poor Mary. There is no comforting arm around her shoulders. They don't invite her to join them again.

They just leave her there in her tearful state. Even the angels ask Mary, "Woman, why are you crying?" offering her no comfort. She responds with the same heartbreaking conclusion. *"They have taken my Lord away,"* she said, *"and*

*I don't know where they have put Him."* Poor Mary is still looking for the wrong Jesus.

What kind of Jesus are *you* looking for: a God who gives you what you want, or a God who only provides what you need, or a God of your own creation, meant to fill in the blanks when life doesn't make sense? Are you searching for a God who will rescue you from life's difficulties, or a God who will save you from yourself? Maybe a deity who slows your fall like a parachute, or a God into whose hands you fall trustingly? Sometimes, we mistakenly believe that God is looking for dependable people. Christ is looking for individuals willing to depend on Him.

This is my Jesus, who left nothing to the imagination when He said, *"...apart from Me, you can do nothing"* (John 15:5). Now we understand why Mary and the disciples feel defeated and hopeless. They believe that Jesus has abandoned them, leaving them confused about what to do next.

After Mary's conversation with the angels, she turns around, and it is written... *she saw Jesus standing there, but she did not realize it was Jesus*. Why didn't Mary recognize Christ? Have you ever bumped into someone you didn't expect to see? Someone out of context? You might even think to yourself, "Hey, that looks like Bill. He could be Bill's twin brother. Wait a minute, Bill, is that you?"

Mary never expected to bump into a *living* Jesus, as she believed He was dead after witnessing His horrific death. She was there until the bitter end. After Christ died, we're told in Mark 15:46-47 that Joseph of Arimathea received Christ's body. It is written, *So, Joseph bought some linen cloth, took down the body, wrapped it in the linen, and placed it*

**in the tomb cut out of rock. Then he rolled a stone against the entrance of the tomb. Mary Magdalene and Mary, the mother of Joseph, saw where He was laid.**

Mary witnessed the gruesome details of Christ's burial. She saw them carry His lifeless body back to the tomb. She watched as they hastily cleaned Him up, carefully pouring spices into the folds of that burial sheet. There was no denying that Jesus was dead and gone. Mary will never forget the scraping sound of the stone being rolled against the entrance of the tomb.

The dull thud of finality, when it dropped into place, shook her to her core. Then Joseph of Arimathea brushed off his hands and stood there for a moment. They all did. Not a word was spoken, as everyone, especially Mary, was horrified by what they witnessed. No one believed that Jesus would come back to life. Not the disciples or Mary Magdalene, no one. Even though Jesus told them repeatedly, **"The Son of Man is going to be betrayed into the hands of His enemies. He will be killed, but three days later He will rise from the dead"** (Mark 9:31 NLT).

They simply didn't believe or understand that this could happen.

Do you believe that Jesus rose from the dead? It seems like a silly question, doesn't it? How you are living your life tells the story if you do. If you're always running scared and feeling overwhelmed and confused by life, it begs the question of whether you truly believe in the power of Christ's resurrection. If you're living a defeated life filled with discouragement and helplessness because you feel victimized by the pressures of daily living, then you have missed the point of Christ's death.

You see, the point of Christ's death is His resurrection. His conquest over sin, death, and the devil is our victory as well. Jesus said, in John 10:10 ESV, *"I came so that they may have life and have it abundantly."*

Not trouble-free living, but lives that are capable of enduring and overcoming the difficulties of life. We read in 1 John 5:4 **for everyone born of God overcomes the world, even our faith.**

This is the victory that has overcome the world, **even our faith.** Jesus' victory over the grave represents *our triumph over all things*.

Did you know that the Greek word for victory is 'Nike'? The goddess Nike had the power to fly. Rumor has it, so did Michael Jordan. His signature shoes were named the Jordan Flight and Air Jordans for this reason.

It's sad that some Christians walk around dragging themselves through life. We need more Christians who are hitting their heads on the ceiling. We are supposed to take flight and soar in victory. We should understand that the power of our faith, which leads to victory, comes from the person we believe in and the kind of Jesus you are looking for. Right now, this same victorious Jesus is standing outside the grave of your troubled life.

Outside the grave of your dead marriage, outside the grave of your mental and physical struggles, Jesus is asking you the same question He asked Mary: *"Who is it that you are looking for?"* Are you looking for a Risen Savior or a fallen hero, murdered by evil men?

Mary had to come to terms with her misconceptions about Christ since she was looking for the wrong Jesus. Even now, she believes she's talking to the gardener, a cemetery worker. She asks him, ***"Sir, if you have carried Him away, tell me where you have put Him, and I will get Him."***

Poor, heartbroken, disillusioned Mary turns away from the living Savior to continue her search. Then Jesus does what only He can do. He pierces the veil of Mary's grief, opening her heart with a single word. He simply says her name, "Mary." Suddenly, the fog of grief lifts, and the heartbreak subsides. It's as if someone suddenly slams on the stadium lights; Mary sees Christ clearly. She rushes forward, embracing Jesus with unchecked emotion. This is where things get interesting. Why does Jesus tell Mary, ***"Do not hold on to Me..."*** Later on, when Jesus encounters Thomas, He tells this disciple to inspect His wounds. Jesus says, ***"Put your finger here; see My hands. Reach out your hand and put it in My side"*** (John 20:27).

So, why does Jesus treat Mary differently by telling her not to hold onto Him? There are two reasons. The latter part of Christ's statement gives us a clue for the first reason: ***"Do not hold to Me, for I have not ascended to the Father."*** Jesus is telling Mary she doesn't have to cling to Him because He's not going anywhere, at least not yet. Besides, Jesus has something for Mary to do. This is a wonderful tribute to Mary, despite her sordid past. It highlights the wonders of grace and the empowerment of faith that elevates her to the key role of messenger for Christ's resurrection. At this point, Mary is the first and only person to have seen the Risen Christ.

Confirming that Mary Magdalene is a redeemed child of God, entrusted with an immediate and significant task to fulfill. ***"Tell the disciples I'm alive."*** Therefore, the next time you think you can't be used by God, remember Mary Magdalene. Despite her troubled past, she plays a key role in getting the disciples back on track. Similarly, the Lord can use you to reach others, not because you're perfect, but because you're not.

Your life should exemplify grace. You are a living testament that God is still in the soul-saving, life-changing business of using people for His glory.

So, what's the second reason Jesus tells Mary not to hang on to Him? The clue comes from how Mary addresses Jesus once she recognizes Him. Mary calls Jesus, *"Teacher."* Yes, Jesus was a teacher, but not anymore. The responsibility of proclaiming the Good News will soon fall to the disciples. Now Christ has moved beyond that role. He is no longer a teacher but the Risen Savior, soon to ascend to Heaven and take His rightful place at the right hand of the Father, becoming the *...one mediator between God and men, the Man Christ Jesus* (1 Timothy 2:5 ESV).

Unfortunately, Mary's bear hug signals that she wants things to return to the way they were. But this is impossible because nothing will ever be the same. Jesus' resurrection changes everything, becoming the gateway to the future. The reason Mary is looking for the wrong Jesus is that she's stuck in the past. Sadly, some Christians are living this way. If you are dwelling in the past, you will miss the present and overlook the future.

Here are four indications that you may be living in the past:

1.  You often talk about how things once were, wishing they were that way again. You don't trust the present, and you're fearful of the future.

2.  You resist change. Technology is the boogeyman you want nothing to do with. Instead of embracing it, you run from it.

3.  You can't escape guilt. You keep blaming yourself for past mistakes instead of forgiving yourself and moving forward.

4.  You are burdened by grudges, holding on to what people have done or said. This keeps you shackled to those past experiences.

So, what's the answer? If you trust God with your future, your past can't hold you back.

Read what the Apostle Paul wrote in Philippians 3:13-14 ESV, **Brothers, I do not consider that I have made it my own. But one thing I do: forgetting what lies behind and straining forward to what lies ahead, I press on toward the goal for the prize of the upward call of God in Christ Jesus.**

Did you catch those key words of Paul, **...forgetting what lies behind and straining forward to what lies ahead.** Here, Paul decides that he won't allow his past to prevent him from embracing his future. He says, **I press on toward the goal for the prize of the upward call of God in Christ Jesus.**

Do you know what the upward calling of God is? It's having a sense of purpose in your life that is God-ordained. It means doing what the Lord placed you on this earth to do. This will provide you with a renewed sense of purpose that everyone needs. If you are a child of God but find yourself floundering in life, then you need to discover this renewed sense of purpose. This is what Jesus gives Mary Magdalene. He tells her, *"Go, Mary…"* (instead of clinging to Me, instead of living in the past,) *"Go… to My brothers and tell them, I am ascending to My Father and your Father, to My God and your God"* (John 20:17).

In other words, tell them, mission accomplished! At that moment, a grieving Mary lets go of Christ, then wipes her tears with the back of her hand and becomes a woman with a mission. Mary has a renewed sense of purpose; that's her upward calling.

Each of us needs to find our upward calling, which means determining why the Lord put us on this planet. For Mary, in that moment, it was, "Go tell my brothers I'm alive." We need to petition the Lord to help us discover our sense of purpose. This will require the courage to obey, accept change, and demonstrate a willingness to do something new. You must become bound and determined to find out what the Lord God has for you to do today and for the rest of your life. This means trusting God with your future so that your past can't hold you back. It won't be an easy road; life never is. However, if we believe, *"For with God nothing will be impossible"* (Luke 1:37 KJV), then those endless possibilities are limited only by our fear and reluctance.

Why not live a "Nike-like" existence, since we serve a victorious and resurrected Savior? It's time to fly, Brothers and Sisters in Christ. It's time to serve our Mighty God with everything you have and everything you are, so that you can do all you can for the Kingdom of God.

## Chapter 10 Questions

1. How would you characterize Mary's emotional state each time she comes to the garden tomb?

2. Why did Mary believe that Christ's remains had been stolen?

3. Mary Magdalene's exorcism is briefly described in Luke 8:1-3. Read the passage and note your thoughts on what her life might have been like during that time.

4. Who did Mary believe stole Christ's remains, and why?

5.  What impact did Christ's death have on His followers? How would you have reacted?

6.  How do we know for sure that Mary was looking for the wrong Jesus?

7.  Do any of the four indicators of living in the past apply to you? How?

8.  Do you believe that if you trust God with your future, your past won't hold you back? What, if anything, is preventing you from moving forward?

# Meet the People Who Met Jesus Today

## Blessings Behind Bars

# Chapter 11
# Dennis

"I'M GLAD YOU'RE HERE," SAID THE DEPUTY. "He's been sitting in the same spot for a long time, not moving, just staring." I walked over and called his name, which seemed to jolt him back to reality. I introduced myself and said, "Let's go talk." I told him people are concerned about him, so I asked what was going on. "I'm drowning," he said. "I'm drowning in guilt and shame."

Dennis is a registered sex offender. He's been through treatment and has been clean for two years. Without thinking, Dennis violated his parole. He called his parole officer right away to confess his infraction. Dennis has a good working relationship with this parole officer, but he was on vacation at the time. So another parole officer stepped in and, without a second thought, had Dennis put back in jail. This is why Dennis is drowning in guilt and shame.

Dennis said, "I need forgiveness, but I don't know where to find it." So I took Dennis to the cross. I talked about how God's forgiveness is made possible through the death and resurrection of Jesus. I told him that God had written John 3:16 with him in mind. "For God so loved the world (Dennis) that He gave His one and only Son, that whoever (Dennis) believes in Him shall not perish but have eternal life."

Suddenly, Dennis wasn't drowning anymore. He was breathing in God's grace instead. He began to realize that while he knew about Jesus, he didn't truly understand how to receive forgiveness through the Savior. So, I introduced him to the King of Kings. Dennis prayed the salvation prayer willingly. I saw his shoulders relax as the tidewaters of guilt and shame ebbed away.

Later, I encountered the same deputy at lunch, who said, "I don't know what you talked about, but he's doing better; he seems to be a new man." "He is," I said, "he really is."

1. Can you think of a sin God can't forgive?


2. How do you feel about God forgiving a sex offender?


3. Guilt and shame are heavy weights to carry around. The only way to find freedom is to go to the Cross. Honest conversation with God is essential to breaking free from those weights. Is a trip to the Cross necessary for you?

# Chapter 12
# **Bruce**

BRUCE'S MESSAGE TO ME WAS SIMPLE AND DIRECT. "I NEED A BIBLE I NEED JESUS." So, I went to lunch. No, I didn't! The Holy Spirit doesn't have to hit me over the head. I grabbed a Bible and hustled over to Bruce's housing unit. I was curious about why he needed Jesus. Bruce explained that his grandmother was a Christian who often took him to a Baptist church when he was a kid. (God bless godly grandmothers!)

Bruce said he had always wanted to be baptized but never got the chance. I explained that baptism is an outward sign of an inner condition, necessary after accepting Jesus as Lord and Savior. I asked Bruce if he had ever surrendered his life to Christ. He paused, not because my question was strange, but because he was wondering why he hadn't given his life to Christ before this moment. "I don't think so," Bruce said, "I guess I should have." So, I shared the Gospel with Bruce. This was something he had heard before but never thought of making it his own. Why not?

How come incarcerated men and women are so willing to turn to God so easily? Is it just jailhouse religion? No, it's not. When you meet someone outside of jail and ask them how things are going, they will usually say "great, good, fine," even when things are not going well. In jail, there is no room for pretense, because things are not great, good, or fine. In jail, everything is a mess, with the potential for serious consequences. Frequently, an inmate will say, "The reason why I'm here is because God wanted to get my attention." I would agree.

It often takes a crisis for us to turn to the Lord for help. When things are going smoothly, we tend to forget about God and make prayer our last resort. This approach always spells trouble, which is God's way of reminding us that prayer should be our first response, NOT our last resort. Bruce said he wanted to get back to God.

His exact words to me were, "I really need Jesus." Don't we all? Not just when we're in trouble, but all the time. I frequently tell the inmates, "The Lord won't force Himself on you, because God wants you to want Him." Bruce finally understood that. This is why he prayed to receive Christ as his Lord and Savior.

After he prayed, I asked him how he felt. With tears in his eyes and a smile on his face, Bruce said he had chills and felt pretty good. I had already given a Bible to a deputy to pass on to Bruce after our meeting. So, I told Bruce to start reading the Gospels. I also encourage inmates to memorize Psalm 23.

At night, when you can't sleep, recite it. It will help you go back to sleep, that's my advice. I find it helpful, and it can work for you too.

1. Have you ever considered how many people attend church regularly yet may not have a relationship with Jesus Christ? What can be done to change that?

2. Saving faith isn't just something you know about; it's an experience that transforms you from the inside out. Have you experienced this kind of spiritual transformation?

3. How often do you share your faith-changing experience with others? Imagine what could happen if you did.

# Chapter 13
# Frank

ONE OF FRANK'S TATTOOS SAID, "STAY WOKE." I admit I was curious, but I focused on his story instead.

Frank told me he began drinking at 8 years old. I don't know how or why; he just did. Along the way, he experimented with other drugs. At the age of 17, Frank went into rehab. He emerged strong and ready to take on life. For the next 10 years, Frank remained clean. He worked hard, fell in love, and had two kids. He bought a 5-bedroom house that made him very proud.

But his marriage started falling apart because he was dabbling with drugs again. Frank's marriage ended when his wife left him. She also abandoned the kids. Frank tried to hold things together, but he couldn't handle the pressure. So, he resorted to his old habits by heavily using drugs. It started to affect his job, which he lost. Consequently, he turned to selling drugs while continuing to use them, trying to survive. Frank admits that next on his list was heroin. But before taking the plunge, he ended up using and fell into a drug stupor. He passed out, hit his head, and began bleeding. When his kids saw the blood, they ran next door. The police were called, and Frank was arrested. He lost his kids, his home, and any hope of holding his life together.

Now Frank is in jail talking to me. He mentioned God, which gave me the opening I had been looking for. He said he grew up Baptist but stopped going to church years ago. So, I asked him my two 'go-to' questions.

Frank had a vague understanding of who Jesus is, but no idea how to answer God. I pointed to Frank's tattoo and told him that he is not 'woke' about Jesus. I said he was asleep to who Jesus really is and why He came. I also told Frank that the Lord put him in jail to wake him up to the Truth. So, I shared the Gospel truth with Frank. That's when Frank's heart woke up from its spiritual siesta. Willingly, Frank prayed to receive Christ as his Lord and Savior. Now he's headed to rehab, hoping to get his kids back. I pray he does.

When Adam fell asleep, he woke up to find Eve standing there. When Frank woke up, he found God standing there. The only difference is that the Lord had been there the whole time.

1. Who is Jesus Christ to you?

2. If you were to die tonight and stand before God, and He were to ask you, "Why should I let you into My Heaven?" what would you say?

3. Do you think Frank can turn his life around, or is it hopeless? Explain your reasoning.

# Chapter 14
# Patrick

A SINGLE ACT CAN CHANGE YOUR LIFE, sending it into a downward spiral, with the ground approaching rapidly. That's where Patrick finds himself. His mugshot reveals tears streaming down his face. He is so distraught that he is immediately placed on suicide watch. Gradually, after a few days, Patrick pulls himself out of his pit of despair. But now he must confront the harsh reality of what he has done. In a fit of rage, Patrick strikes his wife, seriously injuring her. He's arrested, and an order of protection is issued to keep him away. Patrick is overwhelmed with guilt over his actions.

To make matters worse, he has no family in the area, so Patrick believes he's now homeless. He has a job that he might lose and a relationship that may be ending. Patrick asks for a Bible and wants to meet with me. As he sits down, the tears begin to flow. The look on his face indicates he's on the brink of despair.

Can I pull him back? No, but the Lord can. I asked him why he wanted a Bible. Patrick explains that he's not religious, but he had a grandmother who took him to church when he was a kid. Once again, God bless godly grandmothers!

Little does Patrick know that despite all he's lost, he is about to find the greatest treasure in the world. Patrick's mindset is that he has no place to turn. So, it's easy to steer him to the Calvary Cross as I share the Gospel. His reaction? "This makes perfect sense," are his exact words. "How do I do this?" is his next statement. So, I explain how he can. "Can I do this now? Will you help me?" is what Patrick asks me.

I can't express how humbling this moment is. Think of it: God uses us to reach the lost, but only if we are willing and prayerfully express our willingness to lead others to the cross. This morning, I prayed for that opportunity before coming to work, and God answered my prayer. More importantly, Patrick's salvation prayer was heard loud and clear by the Lord Himself. Now Patrick's spiritual journey begins, and he walks away smiling while thanking me for meeting him.

By the way, I know there are people like Patrick in your life. Are you praying for an opportunity to share the Gospel with them? Are you willing to be used by the Lord to lead them to God's soul-saving, life-changing truth? If you don't, who will?

1. Is guilt-inspired shame a bad thing? How would you respond to someone like Patrick?

2. Do you believe that losing everything leads to a hopeless situation?

3. How can the Lord God work in such circumstances?

# Chapter 15
# **Brian**

ARE YOU READY? Ready for what the Lord can do? Are you willing? Willing to turn to God on His terms, not yours? Sometimes the Lord allows life to break us so that He can reshape us. (Read Jeremiah 18:1-6) The winds of change are rarely a gentle breeze; they're more like gale-force gusts. The moment Brian sat down, I could see that he had weathered a personal storm. More than tears, there was a readiness in his eyes. The tears were related to the recent loss of his parents, while the readiness stemmed from his awareness that he needs more of God in his life.

Saving faith is not about rules or rituals; it's about having a relationship with God through His Son, Jesus. If we could save or fix ourselves by following a set of rules or participating in rituals, then why did Jesus live, die, and rise again? Jesus came because rules and rituals cannot save us. Only faith in His work on the cross can. **God did not send His Son into the world to condemn the world, but to save the world through Him** (John 3:17).

This confirms that *everyone* needs a Savior. Brian is aware that within his faith experience, something is missing. He desires more of God because his life has been a series of swings and misses. Genuine faith, saving faith, hinges on a desire to embrace Jesus with unashamed dependence. If you're not *fully* committed to Christ, then there's a gap in your commitment. Brian is ready to mend that gap. The Lord has always been prepared for Brian: prepared to save him and prepared to help him embrace all that He offers.

No one can come to this place of decision unless the Spirit of God brings them. But we never know how or when this will happen. ***The wind blows wherever it pleases. You hear its sound, but you cannot tell where it comes from or where it is going. So it is with everyone born of the Spirit*** (John 3:8).

When the wind blows, be prepared to assist someone across the threshold of God's saving grace. Perhaps this is something you need to do for yourself? Maybe today is the day for you to mend the hole in your spiritual commitment to God. The Lord is always ready to fill in the gaps and smooth out the rough edges. Perhaps it's time to fully devote yourself to God. Are you ready? Are you willing? Brian is. Can you hear the wind blowing?

So, Brian opens his heart, praying for the Lord to forgive and save him, giving him what he's missing. Now, Brian feels complete in his faith experience because he truly is. Do you?

1. Why is saving faith about a relationship with God through Jesus Christ?

2. How would you evaluate your commitment to God? Is it intact or in need of repair?

3. So, is the Wind blowing?

# Chapter 16
# Henry

THE NIGHT AIR IS WARM, prompting people to gather on a neighborhood street. They're talking and laughing when someone notices a car slowing to a stop. The car's windows are open, allowing a man to lean out. Suddenly, shots ring out! Now, people are screaming and running, while tires screech as the car speeds away. Three people are hit by a volley of bullets; one person dies that night on the street.

Hours later, Henry is identified and arrested as the triggerman in this drive-by shooting. Now he's in jail, charged with murder. Henry also learns that his mother has just passed away. When I sit down with him, this street-tough young man of 25 cries over losing his mom. It seems like a cruel twist of fate, doesn't it? But wait. Henry tells me he has fond memories of his mother. Henry's mom was a devoted Christian who took him to church every Sunday. Yes, every Sunday. Thank goodness for godly mothers!

So, I ask Henry who Jesus Christ is to him. He quickly responds, "My Lord & Savior." Then I ask, "If you were to die tonight and God asks you why He should let you into Heaven, what would you say?" Tearfully, Henry responds, after burying his head in his hands, "I don't know. I don't know. I don't know."

Henry doesn't know because he doesn't really know Jesus. He's heard about the Savior but has never put his faith in Him. However, if Henry's dear mother hadn't taken him to church, we wouldn't be talking about who Jesus is and why He came.

I can only imagine how many times Henry's mom prayed for him and how often she worried about the things he was doing since he was hanging out with the wrong crowd. However, this mother's investment of time and love paid off. In her death, Henry found life—eternal life. The example of Henry's godly mother becomes the stepping stone for his salvation experience.

Henry prays and surrenders his life to God, so now he truly knows who Jesus is. This is why we should never stop praying for family and friends who need the Lord.

1. Do you agree that Christian parental influence can have a positive lasting effect on children? How?

2. How, despite Henry's exposure to the Gospel message, does he still not know Jesus personally?

3. Who are the family members you need to pray for? Will you do this regularly?

# Chapter 17
# Marcus

MARCUS' MESSAGE HAD A SENSE OF URGENCY that I've seen before. He wrote, "I need God in my life." Even though this sounds like a slam dunk, I know that things are not always what they seem. Marcus had many questions about being saved, finding forgiveness, and becoming a Christian. He did his homework. I carefully explained the Gospel, fully expecting Marcus to give his life to Christ. And yet, there was something holding him back. Then Marcus asked this: "If I give my life to Christ, will He give what I want?" Some refer to this as 'transactional faith' or making a deal with God. The Lord isn't a celestial Santa Claus, ready to give us what we want. It doesn't work that way.

So, I shared a story with Marcus. It's about a man sitting at a red light, watching people pass by on the crosswalk. Suddenly, the man sees Jesus walking by. He quickly rolls down his window and calls out, "Lord, if it's You, please get in my car. I'll take you wherever you want to go." Jesus walks over to the driver and says, "Son, I don't ride, I drive." It is a simple story that affirms the need to relinquish ourselves to God's control. I told Marcus he needs to slide over and let Jesus take the steering wheel of his life. It wasn't the answer Marcus wanted, so we reached an impasse. I made sure Marcus had a Bible and never heard from him again.

It's easy to get discouraged when people reject the Gospel. Don't assume that your words are seeds falling on barren soil. Only the Lord knows the condition of someone's heart. Our job is to sow the seeds of truth whenever possible, leaving the harvest up to God. The other day, I received a Bible that belonged to Marcus. I know it was his because his name was inside the front cover. Somehow, in the dimly lit confines of his cell or through conversations with other Christian inmates, the Lord reached Marcus. I know this because of what Marcus wrote on the last page of his Bible.

"Dear Lord, I pray you will bless me on my court date to get released to Teen Challenge so that I can better myself and build a closer and stronger relationship with You. I'm ready to give my life and heart over to my Lord and Savior. I know you are shaping my life the way I'm supposed to live. Please take the steering wheel now, my Lord and Savior."

Remember, the Lord is not some distant deity sitting on a faraway throne, but a God with His sleeves rolled up, busy saving and changing lives every day. Please do your part.

1. When it comes to faith issues, some people cry wolf without any real intention of following through. How can you discern who is serious and who isn't?

2. "Jesus, take the wheel" is a common expression suggesting surrender. Is it a legitimate teaching tool? Do you agree that even after becoming a Christian, there is an ongoing need to relinquish control to the Lord? How is it going so far?

3. Not everyone is an evangelist, but every Christian is called to be a witness to the Gospel message. So, how are you fulfilling this responsibility? When Jesus shared the truth, some people resisted. What kind of resistance have you experienced as you shared your faith?

# Chapter 18
# Steve

BLESSINGS BEHIND BARS: PEOPLE FIND LIGHT IN DARK PLACES. It's the light of God's forgiving love breaking through. Steve is a perfect example. He's a Christian who has backslidden. He was an avid churchgoer and a young, talented musician. But a church leader took Steve under his wing, only to sexually abuse him, shattering Steve's life and his faith. This trauma drove Steve into a life of addiction because he wanted to dull the pain. Now at 30, Steve has opened himself to God once again. First, he had to work through several "Why" questions. It's OK to ask God 'why' questions; He can handle them. The most profound 'why' question came from Jesus Himself. **My God, My God, WHY have You forsaken Me?** (Matthew 27:46).

Steve reached out to me and said he wanted to repent of his sins and recommit himself to Christ.

Sometimes, my job feels like I'm filling a glass with clean, cool water and handing it to someone who is dying of thirst. Steve took the glass willingly. He swallowed hard and confessed his sins. He drank slowly but deliberately, taking time to thank the Lord for His forgiveness. When the glass was empty, Steve had prayed to recommit himself to the Lord. I told Steve that now he has even more to offer than music. He has HIS story—a story of heartache and healing. A story that points others to the Lord, no matter where they've been or what they've done. A prodigal story with life-changing power.

I now notice that Steve has a smile that never fades. I can safely say his soul is refreshed. In John 4:14, Jesus said this is available to anyone with a spiritual thirst: ***...but whoever drinks the water I give them will never thirst. Indeed, the water I give them will become in them a spring of living water welling up to eternal life.*** So, drink up!

1. Have you ever felt so far from the Lord that there was no way to get back?

2. If your heart is filled with 'why' questions, how should you handle it?

3. If you're feeling spiritually dry and in need of refreshment, what should you do?

# Chapter 19
# Karl

WHEN A BARRAGE OF BULLETS PELTED HIS CAR, Karl believed that he and his son would die. However, they emerged unscathed from this onslaught. As Karl looked down, he noticed a Bible on the seat between them, having no idea where it came from. Believing and grateful that God had protected them, Karl decided to have an image of Jesus tattooed on his lower leg. This frightening experience moves Karl closer to saving faith by chipping away at the barren, hard soil surrounding his heart.

Much later, a kind and friendly coworker shares his faith with Karl in a way that tills the soil of Karl's heart, preparing it for planting. After another incarceration, Karl connects with an older Christian man and cellmate who reads the Bible aloud while Karl listens in thoughtful silence. This is when the seeds of God's Truth are planted. Today, Karl tells me that when he reads the Bible, he cries, irrigating the Word with his tears and cultivating a potential harvest.

But there is a problem, a barrier: ANGER. Karl says he is filled with rage because of all the pain he has endured. He believes this churning resentment disqualifies him from God's loving forgiveness. Even now, Karl sits tight in his seat, with a hair-trigger temper.

So, I asked him a simple question: "When you go to the doctor, do you go when you're well or sick?" "Sick," Karl says, through clenched teeth.

Similarly, when you come to God, you approach Him when you're sick and hurting. You come to God when the pain feels greater than any cure. You arrive broken and filled with things that only God can heal. Karl, God doesn't want you to approach Him when your life is under control; He wants you to come to Him today because He loves you, and you are worth saving now. You can't fix or save yourself, no matter how hard you try. Only the Lord can do that. God can help you with your anger if you surrender to Him just as you are. "Believe in the Lord Jesus Christ and you will be saved."

Now comes tears and prayerful surrender for Karl, followed by a salvation harvest. Only after the Lord allows life to bring us to the end of ourselves does the journey of faith begin.

1. Have you ever been part of someone's conversion experience? Did it occur all at once, or was it a process?

2. Karl's problem was anger. What other issues can serve as barriers to someone receiving God's saving grace?

3. How would you counsel such a person?

# Chapter 20
# Bible Notes

As a jail chaplain, I typically distribute between 60 and 70 Bibles each month. Occasionally, they are returned to me when inmates leave. Sometimes they have notes written by inmates about spiritual matters. Here are a few examples of those notes:

"Today, I gave my life over to the care of God as I understand Him. I know God is my Savior."

"Stay in the moment with God. He's working out your future."

"If you did it, own it. If it's yours own it.""Christianity is not a religion; it's a born-again experience. I believe in Jesus Christ. He died on the cross for my sins."

"I am sorry, my Father. Please have mercy. 153 months" (Jail time).

"You can't know love without God. Ephesians 4:8""Please heal my fear-based situation. Thank you, Lord, my Savior."

"Everyone has a calling. Pay attention to your calling!"

"Peace, love, forgiveness, mercy. God is good. Thank you for saving me. Amen, Glory to the Lord."

Despite the relational conflict and moral confusion present in our world today, don't lose hope! Even in the darkest places, the light of God's redeeming love shines bright because the Lord God is *still* saving souls and changing lives, one person at a time.

1. Do you believe God continues to work behind the scenes to further His kingdom? Name three examples.

2. Is it reasonable to say that Christianity is not a religion? If so, how would you characterize it?

3. Is it true that everyone has a calling, or does this apply only to those in full-time ministry? What is your calling?

**Why I wrote this book:** When my kids were young, bedtime was the perfect time for storytelling. I would ask them, "Do you want me to read you a story or tell you a story?" They would usually say, "Tell us a story." Stories help us understand life. They describe and explain our experiences. The Bible is a collection of stories. My desire is to encourage my readers to explore each Bible story by searching within and behind the bigger story without compromising the truth. We are born into a story, and our lives give birth to stories yet to come.

**Follow John Cherico on Facebook**
to read more Blessings Behind Bars

**If you'd like to support Chaplain John's jail ministry,
you can send your donation to:**
Good News Global
PO Box 6098
Albert Lea, MN, 56007-6098
Please include: J63-Cherico in the memo line of your check.
Thank you for your support!

# About the Author

**REVEREND JOHN CHERICO** is a licensed pastor with 32 years of experience, serving congregations in Illinois, North Dakota, New York, and Minnesota. In 2018, led by the Lord, he joined Good News Global as a jail chaplain and has served at Hennepin County Jail in Minneapolis for seven years. This facility serves Minnesota's largest county, with about 1.3 million residents and an inmate capacity of 600 to 700. Chaplain John provides religious resources and counseling to inmates of various faiths. With an average stay of eight days, he seizes opportunities for "drive-through evangelism" to share the Gospel of Jesus Christ. The following stories are based on these interactions.

Born and raised in the New York metropolitan area during the New York Yankees' dominance, John spent hours mimicking the batting stances of Mickey Mantle, Roger Maris, and Yogi Berra in stickball games. Despite his Yankee-loving friends, he was a fan of Willie Mays. In 1978, he had a born-again transformation, later graduating from Trinity Evangelical Divinity School in 1983. John was married for over 40 years to his wife, Deb, who passed away in 2016; this book is dedicated to her memory. He has four adult children and five grandchildren. John lives in Maple Grove, MN, hoping this book helps readers encounter Jesus in a fresh way and gain spiritual strength through this impactful experience.